THE BEDFORD SERIES IN HISTORY AND CULTURE

Envisioning America
English Plans for the Colonization of North America, 1580–1640

Edited with an Introduction by

Peter C. Mancall
University of Kansas

D1114233

BEDFORD/ST. MARTIN'S   Boston ♦ New York

For Bedford/St. Martin's
President and Publisher: Charles H. Christensen
General Manager and Associate Publisher: Joan E. Feinberg
History Editor: Niels Aaboe
Developmental Editor: Louise D. Townsend
Editorial Assistant: Richard Keaveny
Managing Editor: Elizabeth M. Schaaf
Production Editor: Ann Sweeney
Copyeditor: Barbara G. Flanagan
Indexers: Phillip Roberts and Peggy Bieber-Roberts
Text Design: Claire Seng-Niemoeller
Cover Design: Richard Emery Design, Inc.
Cover Art: Engraving by Theodor de Bry, based on a drawing by John White.

Library of Congress Catalog Card Number: 94-65208

For information, write: Bedford/St. Martin's, 75 Arlington Street, Boston, MA 02116
(617-399-4000)

ISBN-10: 0-312-09670-4 (paperback)
        0-312-12252-7 (hardcover)
ISBN-13: 978-0-312-09670-0 (paperback)
        978-0-312-12252-2 (hardcover)

Foreword

The Bedford Series in History and Culture is designed so that readers can study the past as historians do.

The historian's first task is finding the evidence. Documents, letters, memoirs, interviews, pictures, movies, novels, or poems can provide facts and clues. Then the historian questions and compares the sources. There is more to do than in a courtroom, for hearsay evidence is welcome, and the historian is usually looking for answers beyond act and motive. Different views of an event may be as important as a single verdict. How a story is told may yield as much information as what it says.

Along the way the historian seeks help from other historians and perhaps from specialists in other disciplines. Finally, it is time to write, to decide on an interpretation and how to arrange the evidence for readers.

Each book in this series contains an important historical document or group of documents, each document a witness from the past and open to interpretation in different ways. The documents are combined with some element of historical narrative—an introduction or a biographical essay, for example—that provides students with an analysis of the primary source material and important background information about the world in which it was produced.

Each book in the series focuses on a specific topic within a specific historical period. Each provides a basis for lively thought and discussion about several aspects of the topic and the historian's role. Each is short enough (and inexpensive enough) to be a reasonable one-week assignment in a college course. Whether as classroom or personal reading, each book in the series provides firsthand experience of the challenge—and fun—of discovering, recreating, and interpreting the past.

Lynn Hunt
David W. Blight
Bonnie G. Smith
Natalie Zemon Davis
Ernest R. May

Preface

In 1580, most English men and women had only hazy notions about North America. By 1640, thousands of them had risked a hazardous ocean crossing because they believed that their lives would be better on the other side of the Atlantic. Some of the migrants succeeded, others failed. Whatever their individual fortunes, they collectively initiated the English settlement of North America, a process that eventually led to the formation of the United States and the virtual destruction of the native peoples of the eastern woodlands.

In the late twentieth century we tend to forget that these historical processes were not inevitable. We assume that the ultimate success of the English was guaranteed from the outset, either because they possessed military might or the backing of a European nation or immunity to the diseases they unwittingly transported across the ocean. And we assume, too, that the Indians had to lose. But events did not have to take place as they did.

This collection of documents gives twentieth-century readers a glimpse of the time when the possibility of colonizing North America was anything but certain. The documents allow us to view colonization from the earliest articulation of the idea and to observe the unfolding process of promotion and persuasion, exploration and discovery. They allow us to recognize the issues that were important to natives and newcomers alike in the late sixteenth and early seventeenth centuries, particularly the aspirations of English writers who hoped that resources and opportunities for work in overseas settlements would provide much-needed cures for the social ills afflicting England. The texts give us insight into the two worlds on either side of the Atlantic—the world of England where poverty, unemployment, and religious persecution were constant realities and the world of the eastern woodlands of North America where Indian peoples inhabited societies based on long-established beliefs regulating religious practice and community norms. The English writers who described the Indians were not trained ethnographers, nor did they generally appreciate Indian cultures; but they nonetheless wrote about Indian beliefs and practices.

One of them, John White, produced a series of drawings that allow us to observe aspects of Carolina Algonquian life before that culture disappeared in the wake of European colonization. These pictures served as the basis for a set of engravings by Theodor de Bry, sixteen of which are included here.

This book contains two parts. The first is an essay that sets the origins of English America in its historical context, with particular attention to the expansion efforts of other European nations, the experiences of the English in Ireland, the development of English settlements in North America, and the relations between the European newcomers and the American natives they encountered. The second part consists of documents dating from 1580 to 1640 that capture the process of colonization from its origins in promotional propaganda to its realization on the shores of North America. The texts reflect changing sensibilities during those two crucial generations from the first tentative attempts to establish an English colony at Roanoke in 1585 to the more sustained efforts of the early seventeenth century. Most important, these documents provide the context for understanding the formation of English colonies and the consequences of overseas expansion for English emigrants and America's indigenous peoples.

By providing insight into the world of the early modern English, this collection of texts allows readers direct access into the workings of a society in the midst of justifying colonization. Exploring the nature of overseas expansion during this period, with an eye to gauging the consequences of colonization for emigrants and Indians, we can get beyond the myths of Jamestown and Plymouth and understand an early modern world through the ideas and actions of those who inhabited it. There can be no surer starting point for any inquiry into the meaning of early American history.

ACKNOWLEDGMENTS

I am grateful to Lou Masur, who provided the initial impetus and the title for *Envisioning America;* to Sabra Scribner, who took an early interest in this project; and to Charles Christensen and Joan Feinberg for having faith that readers in the late twentieth century might be interested in events that took place four hundred years ago. I also want to thank the people at Bedford Books who provided enormous assistance at every stage. Barbara Flanagan was an ideal copyeditor, Ann Sweeney deftly and intelligently guided the book through various stages of its production, and

Mary Lou Wilshaw and Diane Bernard proofread the final volume with great care. I especially want to thank Louise Townsend, whose labors transformed my often random thoughts into a coherent volume that, I hope, lives up to her exacting standards. A number of historians provided close readings of the introductory essay (or its earlier variants) and I am pleased to thank them now: Nicholas Canny, David Cressy, Richard R. Johnson, Mark Kishlansky, Karen Ordahl Kupperman, Lou Masur, Steve Pincus, Ben Schmidt, Timothy Silver, and Alan Taylor. I am forever in debt to Lisa Bitel, who as always spent many hours helping me to complete this work. I dedicate this work to her, and to Nicholas and Sophie, with the hope that the America that they inhabit lives up to their visions of it.

Peter C. Mancall

Contents

PART ONE

Introduction:
English Promotion and
Settlement of the Americas

In 1585, on the eve of the first substantial British efforts to establish colonies in the Western Hemisphere, Richard Hakluyt the elder, a prominent London lawyer, succinctly described the rationale for those efforts. After enumerating the varied rewards, he further stated three goals of colonization:

1. To plant Christian religion.
2. To trafficke.
3. To conquer.

"Or," he added, "to doe [do] all three." (See Document 1.) Hakluyt's statement perfectly captured the essence of English plans for the colonization of North America. Few of the migrants who sailed across the Atlantic Ocean from the 1580s to the 1640s would have disagreed with Hakluyt's assessment.

As Hakluyt himself realized, more than the pursuit of grandeur and profit motivated colonization efforts. Those who promoted overseas settlements were also responding to domestic problems in England. Hakluyt wrote that colonization could help England rid itself of the "offals of our

1

people."[1] Over the next few decades, other writers expressed similar aims, seeing in the colonization of North America both a solution to England's lingering problems and the key to its future.

These promoter's writings, including the selections offered here, shaped the course of early American history by providing explanations and justifications for the English men and women who were attempting to create their "new England" in North America. This was a process of envisioning in its broadest sense. Those involved in it used the information they gathered from promoters in England, and whatever they could learn from American Indians, to initiate the English settlement of eastern North America from the Atlantic to the Appalachian Mountains.

Of course, the lands they wanted to colonize already had people on them. Indians had long inhabited the eastern woodlands of North America by the time English colonists arrived in the late sixteenth century, and perhaps one million of them lived between the Mississippi River and the Atlantic Ocean in 1600.[2] They had well-established economies, based generally on a mix of agriculture and hunting. Most Indian economies were gender-segregated, with women usually tending to the farming chores while men hunted. Though cultural distinctions separated Indian groups, many had established trade relations with others. Further, each group had its own political system capable of maintaining internal order and negotiating with outsiders. Finally, every Indian group possessed its own set of religious beliefs. All of these aspects of the cultures of the eastern woodlands Indians influenced their relations with the Europeans who had come to expand their empires across the Atlantic.

The promoters whose works are included in this collection expressed the earliest English visions of North America and captured some of the first colonial depictions of Indians in what Europeans termed the "New World." Two cousins, each named Richard Hakluyt, edited and published travel accounts in the 1570s and 1580s even though they never saw the territory they wanted English men and women to settle. George Peckham, involved in one of the earliest colonization efforts, speculated about creating a feudal society in the Northeast. Thomas Harriot and John White, leaders of the effort to settle Roanoke (an island off the coast of modern-day North Carolina) in the 1580s, provided remarkable images in words and pictures of the Carolina Algonquian Indian religion. Sir Walter Ralegh, a close associate of Queen Elizabeth, described the riches of Guiana (along the northern coast of South America), an English colonial venture that failed. George Percy, one of the leaders of the Jamestown settlement near Chesapeake Bay (in Virginia), wrote about the horrors that visited the English migrants after the founding of the settlement in 1607; accounts such as his prompted the Virginia Company to offer its own propaganda supporting the colony. The Puritan leader John Winthrop in the 1620s and Captain John Smith in the early 1630s wrote justifications for the continued colonization of North America. William Wood, another Puritan, provided posterity with a careful rendering of the lifestyles of New England's native peoples in the 1630s.

It is tempting to analyze these works from a literary perspective. The earliest writers at times offered extravagant claims for what America had to offer. Trying to create visions with their words, they drew on commonly accepted wisdom and hoary authorities when they described the supposed resources of the Western Hemisphere. They enticed their audiences with portrayals of the fantastic wealth to be gotten through colonization, lacing their tracts with luscious images of almost unimaginable riches. The later promoters who actually visited the Western Hemisphere offered more realistic though no less enthusiastic accounts of North America and the benefits to be derived from colonization there. In the process of trying to motivate English men and women to cross the ocean they created a distinct literature of colonization, a body of venerable texts that would-be migrants could turn to when they contemplated the prospect of leaving the known world behind. To this day we do not know how many people read these works. But the size of their readership does not reflect in any way on their worth. Taken together they constitute a staggering series of writings capable of stirring the imagination. Their images of splendor must have captivated those who read the tales in much the same way that the most notable literature of their age roused men and women to contemplate a world existing beyond the often dreary confines of their communities.

The texts that constitute this literature of colonization are historical documents that need to be understood within their particular historical context. Most important, they need to be seen against a backdrop of what one historian has termed "worlds in motion,"[3] the ubiquitous movements of peoples that were taking place in early modern Europe (from approximately 1500 to 1800). Migration was not a new phenomenon in this period. Europeans had been in the process of migrating for centuries, though their movements tended to be relatively short; any long-distance migrations that occurred typically involved small numbers of people.[4] From the end of the fifteenth to the end of the eighteenth century, however, the scale of migrations increased, especially after the creation of European colonies in the Americas.

English plans for the Americas often had an overoptimistic tone, especially given the hardships experienced by the first colonists, both at Roanoke (where an entire colony, cut off from the support it needed from England, mysteriously disappeared) and in Jamestown. Perhaps that spirit of optimism sprang from the need for promoters of colonization to make persuasive cases to a government that was only marginally interested in overseas settlement. In the world of competing interests and court factions of Elizabethan England, those who wanted government support for their plans knew well that they would have to struggle to get attention.

From the 1580s through the 1630s some promoters succeeded in getting the attention they sought, or at least enough support to mount their ventures. Their tracts became blueprints for colonial expansion, providing guidelines for adventurers and common men and women who struggled to survive in North America. Their struggle paid off in the long run, according to English writers. As the economist Adam Smith wrote in *The Wealth of Nations* in 1776, "the discovery of America, and that of a passage to the East Indies by the Cape of Good Hope, are the greatest and most important events recorded in the history of mankind."[5]

EARLY EUROPEAN SETTLEMENTS IN THE WESTERN HEMISPHERE

For almost a century before the English established colonies in North America, most of the Europeans who ventured westward came from Spain, Portugal, and France. They hoped to spread Catholicism wherever they went in the "New World" and to profit from shipping the natural resources of the Americas to Europe. The experiences of these Europeans proved vital to later English promoters, who encouraged English settlement of North America by demonstrating the success of previous transatlantic ventures. Further, the English feared that any success enjoyed by these Catholic nations could lead to danger both at home and on the seas.

Following Christopher Columbus's voyages in the 1490s, the Spanish sent wave after wave of conquistadors westward, through the Caribbean to Mexico, southward into South America, and northward into what is now the southwestern United States. Their exploits were often bloody—perhaps none more so than Hernando Cortés's conquest of the Aztecs from 1519 to 1521 and Francisco Pizarro's assault on the Incas during the late 1520s and early 1530s—but the Spanish also claimed religious motivations. As one early chronicler declared, the Spanish sought "to bring light to those in darkness, and also to get rich, which is what all of us men commonly seek."[6] Though the English eventually criticized Spanish treatment of American Indians, few Europeans would have denied the success

of these colonizers. By the end of the sixteenth century, Spanish con-
quistadors, notably Francisco Coronado, had traveled extensively through
North America, and Spanish settlements stretched from present-day New
Mexico to Chile.

Spain's colonization of Central America and parts of South America
demonstrated that the meeting of Europeans and Native Americans had
unimaginable and irreversible consequences, especially for the Indians.
When the Spaniards moved across the Atlantic, they became the first
Europeans to unleash deadly diseases among the native peoples of the
Americas. The Spanish had no notion that the germs they carried, particularly smallpox, could have a horrific impact on Native Americans. They
could not have known that those peoples inhabited a world free of Eurasian
diseases and thus had no immunities to them. The Spanish suffered little
from the germs they carried, since they had developed immunities to them
in childhood. But those germs created epidemics that devastated Indian
communities in the Americas. Within a few generations, with illness
spreading from seemingly every European ship and often transported
along indigenous trade routes, the aboriginal population had decreased by
perhaps 90 to 95 percent. Though military hostilities contributed to the
loss of life, epidemic disease was the greatest cause of death for Indians.

This spread of illnesses was one part of the "Columbian exchange," the
term that historians use to describe the passing of biological matter
between Native Americans and Europeans. That exchange had other
effects as well. Europeans who traveled to the Americas found new foods,
notably potatoes, tomatoes, and squash, which soon became widespread
in Europe. Further, Europeans transported their domesticated live-
stock—cows, horses, sheep, and pigs—to the Americas, where the animals fared remarkably well (although this too had unfortunate consequences for many Indians when these Old World animals destroyed
Indian fields). Eventually, many Indian groups incorporated these species
into their economies and daily lives, but it was Europeans who benefited
most from the exchange.[7]

While Europeans took advantage of the Western Hemisphere's resources and shipped them back to Europe, they were aware that Indians
were dying. During the sixteenth century, the Spanish did not celebrate
the destruction of America's peoples, though they contributed to the death
toll by forcing Mexico's Indians onto marginal lands and making them pay
tribute to the new rulers of Central America; the enslavement of countless
Indians and the savage work regimes in silver mines contributed to the
loss of life as well. But out of the horrors of colonization in New Spain
came one of the most effective critiques of European expansion: the

report of the Dominican missionary Bartolomé de Las Casas entitled *Brevísima relacíon de la destrucción de las Indias [A Short Account of the Destruction of the Indies]*, a "hair-raising catalogue of atrocities," as one historian termed it, recounting in graphic detail the mistreatment of the Indians.[8] The report, subsequently translated into English, later provided justification for Elizabethan efforts to establish colonies in the Americas. The English often claimed that they treated Indians more fairly than the Spanish did. It is thus not surprising to find that Sir Walter Ralegh himself cited Las Casas's report in his description of his attempts to establish an English colony in Guiana near the end of the sixteenth century.[9]

Reports of alleged Spanish atrocities enraged many English Protestants but such stories did not, by themselves, lead to any desire to migrate to the Americas. A more important motivation for colonization came in the circulation within Europe of reports based on the discoveries of explorers. Peter Martyr d'Anghiera, an Italian historian who served as chronicler for the Spanish crown, took reports directly from anyone returning from the Americas (including Columbus) and wrote them up for an audience eager to discover what had been found in the Western Hemisphere. Peter Martyr's work, which began to appear as early as 1516, was collected as *De Orbe Novo* in 1530 and was subsequently translated into other languages, including English, before the end of the century.[10] Based on firsthand information, these writings described the resources of the Americas, or at least those parts explored by Spaniards, thus encouraging other European ventures.

Aware of the successes of the Spanish, the Portuguese and French eagerly sought to profit from overseas expansion. For a time in the sixteenth century, the Portuguese, like other Europeans, searched for the mythic Northwest Passage, a water route through the North American continent that would allow more rapid contact with Asia than the traditional route around Africa. Although they failed to locate this passage, the Portuguese colonized extensively and successfully in Brazil, where the production of sugar eventually generated great profits. Since they concentrated their efforts in South America, these immigrants from the Iberian peninsula encountered little direct competition from the English, and the promoters of English settlements paid relatively little attention to them.

The English paid greater attention to French efforts at colonization. French explorer Jacques Cartier's reports from his explorations in the Canadian northeast in the 1530s testified to an early interest in North America. And well before the English sent colonists across the Atlantic, the French were already busy trying to establish settlements in Florida, a venture they eventually abandoned in the mid-1560s after a violent encounter with the Spanish (who, by the Treaty of Tordesillas in 1494, had the authority to claim much of eastern North America).[11] Even before the end of the sixteenth century, French colonizers were concentrating their efforts on the St. Lawrence Valley, territory that now defines part of the border between the United States and Canada.

Unlike the English, who have left detailed plans about why they established colonies, the French were apparently more reticent. Still, surviving evidence suggests that their motives were similar to those of the English. According to René de Laudonnière, who wrote a history of the expedition to Florida in 1576, the French went to America for two reasons. First, they had "the naturall desire" to "search out the commodities to live happily, plentifully, and at ease." To do so, either they needed to send French people abroad "to dwell in a better" land or they had to find and transport the best resources of the Americas back to France to improve people's lives there. But they had another reason as well: overpopulation. According to Laudonnière, many French people "no longer able to dwell in their native soyles, have entred upon their neighbours limites, and oftentimes passing further have pearced even unto the uttermost regions." Such motivations proved more than sufficient cause for establishing colonies, though Laudonnière warned his readers that the French should not send too many colonists abroad lest they so weaken the home country that it become vulnerable to attack. This was no idle threat to the French, or to any European people, he argued, because the experience of ancient Rome demonstrated that an overextended empire could be toppled too easily.[12] Later promoters, notably the explorer Samuel de Champlain, who wrote about his voyages to Canada in the 1610s, pointed more optimistically to the commercial benefits that had accrued to the ancient Romans, as well as to the Venetians, when they expanded their horizons. Champlain knew well the possible profits of the fur trade, as well as the potential for converting the Indians of the interior parts of North America to Christianity.[13] These twin goals of profit and the spread of Catholicism became the central features of the seventeenth-century French colonization of "New France."

In spite of promoters' efforts, the French never matched the English effort to transplant large numbers of people to North America. Conditions in France might have been bleak, but French men and women for the most part refused to brave the Atlantic crossing to try their luck in Canada.[14] In this sense, the French experience anticipated the colonization efforts of the Dutch who, following in the wake of Henry Hudson's voyage of 1609 (up the river that now bears his name), believed that New Netherlands (which became New York in the 1660s) was a more likely trade outpost than a region suitable for large-scale settlement.[15] For the English, the expansion of the European powers into the Western Hemisphere appeared ominous. During the sixteenth century, the English were dependent on southern European nations for the dyes and oils needed to produce textiles.[16] If those nations became stronger through colonization, their newfound wealth could upset the balance of trade in Europe, with potentially devastating consequences for the English economy. Perhaps more important, in the sixteenth century Protestantism became the dominant religion in England. Though religious tensions would divide Protestants during the seventeenth century and contribute to the Puritan migration to New England, the primary religious tensions before 1600 centered on the conflict between Protestants and Catholics. Under Queen Elizabeth I, an ardent believer in the need to expand the power of Protestants and limit the power of the Catholic Church, Spanish and French efforts to spread Catholicism across the Atlantic constituted a threat that had to be stopped.

EARLY INFLUENCES ON ENGLISH COLONIZATION EFFORTS

The English were not completely without colonizing experience when they reached North America in the late sixteenth century. For generations, perhaps as long as a century, the English had been gathering information about the Western Hemisphere from fishing vessels that sailed west from Bristol. Though documentation for the late fifteenth century is frustratingly thin, reports dating from the venture of John Cabot to Newfoundland in 1497 as well as scattered references to earlier voyages testify to long-standing English navigation of American waters.[17] English explorers had been traveling around the Atlantic since the voyages to the West Indies of Sebastian Cabot and Sir Thomas Pert in the 1510s. Subsequent voyages, of John Hawkins in the 1560s and especially Francis Drake in the 1570s, also demonstrated the potential of long-distance travel. While these explorers' ventures did not lead to colonization efforts, they did indicate interest on the part of the English in overseas expansion. By the mid-sixteenth century, the experiences of these early English explorers combined with reports of European colonization efforts led some Englishmen to consider the potential for planting English colonies in North America.

At that time, those interested in establishing settlements across the Atlantic could also have read one of the most forthright justifications for colonization then available: Thomas More's *The Best State of a Commonwealth and the New Island of Utopia*, first published in 1516. In his description of a mythical island society, More noted that its inhabitants, the Utopians, actively engaged in colonization. They "enrolled citizens out of every city and, on the mainland nearest them, wherever the natives have much unoccupied and uncultivated land, they found a colony under their own laws. They join with themselves the natives if they are willing to dwell with them. When such a union takes place, the two parties gradually and easily merge and together absorb the same way of life and the same customs, much to the great advantage of both peoples. By their procedures they make the land sufficient for both, which previously seemed poor and barren to the natives." If the natives resisted, then the Utopians could "wage war against them. They consider it a most just cause for war when a people which does not use its soil but keeps it idle and waste nevertheless forbids the use and possession of it to others who by the rule of nature ought to be maintained by it."[18]

English promoters of colonization shared this belief that it was their right to colonize lands inhabited by peoples who were living apparently without civilization. To justify their arguments, they drew on the most established ancient writers as well as other eminent authorities. But those authorities, at least to some promoters of colonization, suggested a different scenario than More's optimistic notion that natives and newcomers might coexist in peace. A more pessimistic view emerged in the writings of at least one promoter who had experience with English colonization efforts in Ireland. Sir William Herbert, a colonial administrator and landholder in Ireland, cited the ancient writers Thucydides, Livy, Tacitus, Sallust, and Plato in his defense of colonization schemes, *Croftus Sive de Hibernia Liber*, written in the early 1590s. He paid particular attention to the more recent fifteenth-century Italian political philosopher Niccolò Machiavelli, quoting approvingly from *The Prince*. All these sources led Herbert to issue an unequivocal warning to any potential colonizers who dared to mix with the indigenous population. "Colonies degenerate assuredly when the colonists imitate and embrace the habits, customs, and practices of the natives," he wrote. "There is no better way to remedy this evil than to do away with and destroy completely the habits and practices of the natives. Thus the natives will put on and embrace the habits and customs of the colonists. It will then come about that, once you have removed those things which can alienate hearts and minds, they will both become united, first in habits, then in mind."[19] Absent from such a vision was the sense that colonizers and the colonized would each prosper through any sharing of their cultures.

THE ENGLISH COLONIZATION OF IRELAND

The English attempts to establish settlements in Ireland demonstrated that Herbert's ideas rested on actual experience. The Anglo-Normans had a long history of colonizing other peoples. Their movements to the west and north, beginning in the decades after the Norman Conquest in 1066, took them into Wales and Scotland as well as Ireland and provided ample experience with the tactics necessary for expansion.[20] By the mid-sixteenth century, retaining control of Ireland had become a formidable problem. The Anglo-Normans left to control affairs in Ireland in the twelfth century soon mixed with the native population through intermarriage and cultural conversion; by the early modern period these so-called Old English were, in many ways, indistinguishable from many of the native Irish, at least to English eyes. Beginning in the sixteenth century, the Crown eagerly sought to subdue the native (Catholic) Irish, first by waging a savage military campaign and later by transplanting large numbers of Protestants to Ireland. While the English had economic goals in mind when they battled the Irish in the 1560s—they wanted to keep the economy in a primitive state and thus dependent on England for manufactured goods—the war demonstrated the willingness of the English to shed blood for political goals. Even the use of terror against the civilian population became acceptable in the effort to convince the native Irish that they should capitulate to English rule.[21]

In the aftermath of that mid-sixteenth-century campaign, many English men and women began migrating across the Irish Sea. Approximately four thousand people moved to Munster in the southwest of Ireland in the late sixteenth century. This transplanted population grew to twenty-two thousand in the 1630s, and by 1640 or so Munster's architecture and economy resembled those of England. By the late 1630s, merchants had created stable trade networks, with the English shipping wool to Ireland in exchange for cattle. The colonization of Munster was largely peaceful (until an uprising in 1641–42). More important, the creation of this English colony led to an expansion of markets for English goods and the growth in imports of desirable commodities.[22]

The English learned valuable lessons about colonization from their experiences in Ireland. Given enough time, they reasoned, settlements could eventually be made profitable even if they needed military force to subdue the natives. With patience, even a seemingly primitive people like the Irish could be integrated into the commercial system of the Crown. Further, the English believed that even religious differences could be overcome and the forces of Catholicism turned back. The lessons of the English experience in Ireland were readily available to those engaged in transatlantic settlement schemes.

DOMESTIC INFLUENCES ON EARLY ENGLISH PLANS FOR COLONIZING NORTH AMERICA

By the mid-sixteenth century, when the Elizabethan conquest of Ireland was in full sway, social turmoil beset English society. In particular, population growth threatened to undermine the existing social order. The English government and would-be reformers did not know how to cope with the growing numbers of people, and they struggled to find places to put people to work so that they would not cause disorder.

The population of England soared from approximately 3.25 million around 1570 to 4.07 million in 1600,[23] although it did not reach the levels it had attained before the devastations of the Black Death in the mid-fourteenth century. Simultaneous with the population growth came a change in the agrarian economy of the realm. In particular, landlords enclosed their lands to create large pastures for sheep. This movement encouraged the severing of customary and legal ties between farming families and those who owned the land and caused many rural dwellers, one-time farmers, to look for work elsewhere in England.[24]

Since farming villages could no longer provide sufficient resources for their populations, many inhabitants had little choice but to leave. Though short-distance, mostly seasonal migrations had taken place earlier and were a regular feature even in European societies with stable economies, the scale of migrations within England (as on the continent) became far larger in the sixteenth and seventeenth centuries.[25] The large number of migrants upset the social order. During the latter half of the sixteenth century, those in pursuit of work caused terror for the leaders of a society where poverty, at least among the able-bodied, was a sign of moral degeneracy. Pamphlet writers, government officials, and social observers began to lament, with differing degrees of accuracy, the growth in numbers of people whom they termed "vagrants."

Vagrants, according to sixteenth-century definitions, were far different from poor people in general. To be a vagrant was to be an itinerant able to work but without regular income; those who fit the bill were also presumed to be dangers to society because they spread disease, were idle, and lacked the guidance of a master. Many vagrants were children, often illegitimate or the victims of parental neglect; others were adults who simply could not find work.

Yet while historians can see vagrants as lost wanderers in a changing economy, contemporaries were not so forgiving. Rumors abounded that vagrants traveled the countryside in packs, attacking upstanding citizens and engaging in illicit sexual relations whenever possible. Pamphlet writers even claimed that vagrants were associates of Satan. The popularity of such tracts suggests that many people in early modern England believed these itinerants to be a serious threat to the stability of their society.[26]

Vagrants' poverty made them suspect; their visibility transformed them into objects of fear. Earlier, in medieval England as elsewhere in Europe, beggars had performed a vital social function for those higher on the social scale: Giving charity to the indigent became a way to demonstrate one's Christian goodwill, especially since the holy were often destitute. But the ideological function of poverty began to change in the late Middle Ages and the changes intensified after the Reformation, especially with the dissolution of monasteries in England in the early sixteenth century. Their wealth depleted, churches in England could no longer provide sufficient charity for the poor. By the Elizabethan period, the public generally shunned the seemingly idle poor, although charity enabled many of the wanderers to keep from starving.[27]

Cut off from their traditional means of support, the increasingly numerous vagrants drifted about the countryside in the latter decades of the sixteenth century seeking seasonal employment. Failure led most to search for work in towns. Eventually, thousands of the poor made their way to London. The population of London soared from 120,000 in 1550 to 200,000 in 1600; by 1650, the population of the city reached 375,000. Still unable to find adequate income, the migrants swelled the poor rolls of the city, tripling the number of those requiring relief from 1550 to 1600, with the more fortunate ones who obtained some kind of assistance putting strains on existing charitable institutions.[28] Domestic efforts to solve the problem, including incarceration of the poor in attempts to reform them, failed entirely.[29]

It was at this point, during the late 1570s and early 1580s, that some Englishmen began to believe that establishing colonies in North America could solve the problems created by population growth. The solution was deceptively simple: Send the unemployed across the Atlantic. Having only limited information about the resources of North America, those who promoted colonization during these years presumed that English men and women who traveled across the ocean would be able to create a replica of English society free of the problems that threatened the nation. The English did not always believe that North America was an ideal target; surviving documents from the mid-sixteenth century suggest possible English interest in the Amazon (an interest that became more obvious in the seventeenth century).[30]

Early plans for colonizing North America also emerged in England in the 1570s in response to a growing interest in long-distance commerce. English economic essayists became infatuated with the experience of the Dutch, who they felt had created a wealthy commercial empire even though they were not blessed with great natural advantages; profits from shipping seemed to account for the Dutch riches.[31] In addition, the creation of English trade companies to carry out commerce to the east—to Russia in the 1550s, to the eastern Mediterranean by the 1580s, to India by the end of the century—demonstrated that elite merchants in London were in the process of embracing long-distance trade. These ventures brought such luxuries as currants, silk, and spices to England and, oftentimes more important, opened new markets for English cloth abroad.[32]

In this moment of expanding commercial horizons, promoters argued that the wandering poor should be transported across the Atlantic. The logic of doing so seemed patently clear. "[A] great number of men which do now live idly at home, are burdenous, chargeable, and unprofitable to this realm," Sir Humphrey Gilbert wrote in the early 1580s; sent abroad they could be "hereby set on work."[33] Gilbert, among the most active promoters of colonization until his death in 1583, envisioned himself ruling over a vast American estate peopled with, among others, poverty-stricken English migrants who would produce raw goods for the expanding European market and benefit themselves from the venture. In these late decades of the century still other promoters of overseas settlements routinely offered plans to fill the colonies with the poor, including children.[34]

The two Richard Hakluyts, who spent most of their adult lives in England and cobbled together reports of the potential riches to be found in America, embraced the idea of sending destitute English men and women to overseas settlements. They did so with much greater sympathy toward the plight of the poor than other writers who too easily demonized vagrants. Richard Hakluyt the younger wrote in the preface to his first important published work, *Divers Voyages Touching the Discovery of America and the Ilands Adjacent* (London, 1582), that the English should "beholde with the eye of pitie" their prisons filled with criminals who were to be executed even for minor thefts. It was better, he argued, to send these people to "those temperate and fertile parts of America."[35]

He pursued similar logic in his lengthy work known as the "Discourse of Western Planting" (see Document 2), written in 1584 and distributed among high government officials, including Queen Elizabeth. Hakluyt here noted that the idle and dangerous poor still abounded despite various statutes aimed at reducing the problem of vagrancy. Once transplanted, he argued, the poor could produce desirable commodities for the English market: preparing masts, pitch, tar, and rosin for the shipping trade; planting sugar cane; digging for valuable minerals; tilling for food crops and dyestuffs such as woad and madder. Like those busy establishing what they termed "projects" within England to create work for the unemployed and to produce goods for the market, Hakluyt believed that profits would naturally follow the reorganization of the labor supply.[36] The logic was unmistakable. In order to yield profits, resources had to be developed. Put to work, the idle poor would no longer be idle. They would thus pose no real danger to an emerging English society on the other side of the Atlantic. And in producing goods the English were currently importing from Catholic adversaries in Europe, the colonists would protect the textile economy of England as well.

Early promoters such as the Hakluyts believed that colonies would do more than solve the vagrant problem and enhance the English economy. The Hakluyts claimed that establishing settlements in North America would enable the English to spread Protestantism to America's Indians, find a water route to Asia, and provide strategic support—notably a greater ability to protect English ships—for the English colonization of Ireland. George Peckham, who wrote a pamphlet describing a planned settlement near Narragansett Bay (in modern-day Rhode Island), went further in *A True Reporte of the Late Discoveries . . . by . . . Sir Humphrey Gilbert,* published in 1583 (see Document 3). The report, which emerged in spite of Gilbert's apparent drowning at sea (or because his support-ers needed to prove the lure of their planned settlement even in the wake of his death) noted the possibilities for trading with Indians in the Northeast. He stressed that the English and Indians alike would profit from this exchange. Peckham's plan for a northern trading economy cer-tainly made sense since English fishing fleets had for decades made contact with northeastern Algonquian Indians. But the English migrants who went to North America were not, in Peckham's opinion, to create a simple trade outpost. Peckham hoped to re-create a traditional feudal social order there, with those who invested heavily in the project receiving legal as well as economic powers over other settlers.

There can be no denying that Peckham's plans, like those of the Hakluyts, contained inaccurate assessments of the potential for English colonies in eastern North America. However misguided, these reports revealed the hopes of the earliest would-be colonizers. By the late 1580s, other promoters, some of whom traveled across the Atlantic themselves, pushed the English colonization of North America to the next stage.

THE EMERGENCE OF ENGLISH AMERICA, 1588–1620

From the late 1580s to the 1610s, English plans for colonizing North America evolved in response to increasing information about North America. During these decades English settlers made more consistent efforts to establish overseas plantations, largely because of new government policies toward colonization. By the time this phase of colonization concluded, the English had successfully planted what became their first permanent settlements in North America.

During the 1580s, Queen Elizabeth supported colonization ventures only if they did not detract from what she believed was the primary purpose of her government: to defend the nation and its territory and to consolidate royal authority within the realm. She was much more concerned with preventing invasions of Scotland and Ireland and protecting the English Channel against the Armada, the Spanish fleet that threatened English ships on the high seas.[37] But her government's hesitance ebbed after the English gained access to the seas with their seemingly miraculous victory over Spain in 1588. From that point on, the conditions were ripe for colonizing North America.

In the wake of the defeat of the Armada, promoters redoubled their efforts to establish English colonies in the Americas. In 1587, virtually on the eve of the battle, Richard Hakluyt the younger published an edition of Peter Martyr's work, demonstrating that he, like Martyr himself, best served the cause of the empire by publicizing explorers' texts rather than garnering knowledge through his own ventures. Two years later, Hakluyt published the first edition of his *Principall Navigations,* a collection of explorers' accounts greatly expanded since he had published *Divers Voyages* seven years earlier. The new edition contained the glowing report of Arthur Barlowe, an associate of Sir Walter Ralegh who had traveled along the coast of what is now North Carolina in 1584. Barlowe could not believe what he saw on his journey: North America was a paradise, abundant with natural resources; the land itself seemed to invite colonization. What is more, the natives were friendly. "We found the people most gentle, loving, and faithful," he reported to Ralegh, "void of all guile and treason and such as lived after the manner of the Golden Age. The earth bringeth forth all things in abundance as in the first creation, without toil or labor."[38]

Barlowe was not alone in his assessment of the region. Ralegh held a royal patent to the area giving him control over any English settlements there. In the 1580s he organized voyages for Roanoke, thus initiating the first substantial English efforts to establish settlements on mainland North America. English goals for Roanoke were clear from the start: The settlement would be an ideal staging ground for privateering voyages to rob Spanish ships. Fueled by this idea, an expedition of seven ships left Plymouth in April 1585 and arrived at Roanoke two months later after a harrowing passage across the Atlantic. Initial success in privateering only confirmed the function of the settlement. No one could have predicted that Roanoke would eventually gain its fame from its disappearance by the end of the 1580s.[39]

We know the ultimate fate of the Roanoke effort, but in the 1580s Roanoke seemed an ideal place to begin the English colonization of North America. The importance of the project was evident with the emergence of perhaps the most important work demarcating the emphases of the times: Thomas Harriot's *A Briefe and True Report of the New Found Land of Virginia* (see Document 4). This account established a model for a new sort of reportage based on more exact information about North America. Though he had not yet become the famous mathematician and scientist that he would eventually be, Harriot demonstrated his analytical acumen in his account of the varied resources that existed in Roanoke. He did so with a naturalist's eye, carefully cataloging the flora and fauna of the region. Harriot strove for accuracy since he believed that fantastic claims raised expectations too high and could endanger actual colonization ventures if any colonist returned to England and told tales far different from those contained in the promotional literature.[40] Those who supported colonization knew they had a good thing in Harriot's report. After an initial printing in 1588, it appeared in a 1590 edition that included Flemish printer Theodore de Bry's engravings of the paintings of John White (see Document 4), who had accompanied Harriot to the colony. The 1590 edition appeared almost simultaneously in four languages, testifying to the widespread European interest in America.

By the time the *Report* was published, English men and women already had some idea of what Indians were like. As early as 1501 or 1502, two North American Indians appeared in London, though their inability to communicate with the English and the minimal reporting of their venture limited their importance in the metropolis. Their visit, along with the transport of some Indians to Portugal in 1501 (where they were sent as slaves) and to France in 1509 were only the first of many visits by natives of North America to Europe.[41]

More important than these visits was the publication of reports from Spanish ventures that had circulated in England, especially Las Casas's report, as well as visual representations of the inhabitants of the Western Hemisphere that appeared during the sixteenth century. These images, printed in books, often depicted naked Indians, usually engaged in acts that were intended to highlight their barbarous character for European eyes. Since Europeans during the early modern period tended to dress modestly, images of Indians strolling about partially or completely nude immediately branded them a primitive people. Perhaps such portrayals also suggested a condition of life similar to that prevailing in Africa, with which the English had familiarity long before they crossed the Atlantic for North America. Further, Indians in these pictures often appeared proud, displaying no sense of modesty about either their nakedness or their actions. An expression of defiance, especially on male faces, tended to accentuate the notion that the natives of the Americas were a haughty people.[42]

Harriot's *Report* presented a far different view. Before going to America, Harriot had learned Carolina Algonquian from two Indians, Manteo and Wanchese, who had traveled to England in 1584 with earlier explorers. Possessing this knowledge, Harriot was able to learn more about Indian society in Roanoke than was virtually any other promoter. Perhaps it was his facility with the native language that enabled Harriot to portray Indians in more realistic and sympathetic ways than his predecessors had done. In the *Report,* the natives of Carolina possessed a set of religious beliefs that, though "farre from the trueth," as he noted, nonetheless suggested that the Indians "may be the easier and sooner reformed."[43] Harriot was no uncaring aggressor bent on the Indians' destruction. As his writing made clear, he felt compassion for the Indians when their numbers dropped in an epidemic. He also paid attention to the Indians' views of English colonizers, and by doing so he has left us vital evidence of the Indians' efforts to understand the arrival of both Europeans and their Old World diseases.

The text of Harriot's *Report* gave to English men and women a more sophisticated version of America's Indians, and so did the illustrations that appeared in the 1590 edition of the book. White's pictures gave a far more accurate impression of life in North America than some of the more fantastic visual images conjured up by book illustrators earlier in the century; de Bry's engravings closely followed White's paintings, though with slight alterations, such as making the Indians' faces look more European.[44] To be sure, the heavily tattooed and scantily clad Indians in these images were decidedly un-European in appearance. But other illustrations, notably of the town of Secoton (see page 98), revealed a social order that might have seemed familiar to anyone who traveled through an agrarian village in the English countryside. Taken together, de Bry's engravings of White's pictures suggested that Indians needed reforming but that they were already capable of living orderly lives. To promoters, these Indians seemed perfect for conversion: technologically backward and ignorant of proper religion, but capable (and quite possibly interested in) integrating European wares, and perhaps Christianity, into their daily lives.

The *Report* also included other pictures by White, and these too had a specific message. Significant among these works, most of them redone faithfully by de Bry for Harriot's *Report,* were pictures of Picts, the legendary ancient inhabitants of the British Isles. These Old World images showed Picts acting and looking as the British believed Picts had acted and looked: fearsome. One shows a naked Pictish man, heavily tattooed, holding a human head still dripping blood (see page 104). Two others show Pictish women, similarly naked and tattooed, brandishing spears (see one example on page 106). In case any reader could not grasp the point of including Picts in a work detailing the inhabitants of North America, the text noted that the painter meant to "showe how that the Inhabitants of the great Bretannie have bin in times past as sauvage as those of Virginia."[45]

Here, then, was the point of White's paintings and of Harriot's inclusion of them in his *Report*: although the images depicted savages, they also suggested that the Indians' primitive ways need not survive. If Picts once threatened Britain but had ultimately become subdued and incorporated into the dominant population, so too could the Indians of America. Savagery in this view was not a permanent condition but a transitory stage in the development of any people; under the proper tutelage even the most savage people could become, over time, the most civilized.[46]

In the decade after Harriot's *Report,* more works on the Americas appeared in England. Ralegh published *The Discoverie of the Large, Rich, and Beautiful Empire of Guiana* in 1596 and apparently wrote "Of the Voyage for Guiana" (see Document 5) in the same period. The latter account informed his readers that the English could claim central American territory rich in gold and simultaneously strike a blow against the Spanish who dominated the region. Ralegh was no stranger to the colonization business since he had, like other promoters, firsthand experience in Ireland. But unlike Harriot, Ralegh included information about resources he never saw, particularly mineral wealth. Guiana seemed perfect for English settlement, he believed in the 1590s when he wrote his tract. But try as he might, he never succeeded in creating an English colony there. Instead, he became a victim of the shifting politics of the early seventeenth century when King James I, in an effort to maintain peace with Spain, prosecuted Ralegh for claiming territory in the midst of Spanish possessions in North America. In the end, Ralegh's continued obsession with Guiana led to his execution.[47]

Failure in Roanoke and Guiana did little to stop the flow of information available in England about colonization. At the end of the century Hakluyt brought out an expanded version of his *Principall Navigations,* this time in three volumes (London, 1598–1600). This latest collection included travel accounts dating to the sixth century, with excerpts from King Canute (the Danish king of England around the turn of the millennium) and the fourteenth-century English poet Geoffrey Chaucer; Crusaders' writings about their journeys to the Holy Land (including Richard I's twelfth-century efforts to rescue Jerusalem from the Saracens); reports of travels in Russia and Turkey and throughout the Mediterranean world; and numerous reports from sixteenth-century explorers traveling throughout the Atlantic. Hakluyt's was a magisterial performance, one of the great publishing achievements of the Elizabethan world. Even Shakespeare himself apparently drew on Hakluyt in writing *Macbeth,*[48] and he demonstrated an interest in overseas colonization in *The Tempest,* which was performed for the first time in 1611.

During these decades, English promoters refined the religious arguments for colonization. In their tracts, writers often provided a scriptural justification for their ideas. They were not the first to claim a higher authority. Thomas More had done so in *Utopia* and George Peckham used similar rhetoric in his description of Humphrey Gilbert's venture to Newfoundland (see Document 3).[49] After 1588, such justifications were a vital part of promotional and descriptive tracts. Hakluyt the younger claimed in the Epistle Dedicatory to the first edition of his *Principall Navigations* that Hakluyt the elder had encouraged him to promote colonization in part by citing Psalm 107, "where I read," he recalled, "that they which go down to the sea in ships, and occupy the great waters, they see the works of the

Lord and his wonders in the deep &c."[50] Such logic remained in place for decades, eventually gaining its greatest force during the Puritan migration of the 1630s.[51]

Religion provided only one justification for establishing colonies in North America, as promoters knew well at the turn of the seventeenth century. They also drew inspiration from further commercial expansion. By 1600 or so, English merchants, themselves more inclined to invest in overseas ventures than their sixteenth-century counterparts, received greater encouragement from the government in London than had earlier promoters of colonization. They also realized that pooling their resources in joint-stock companies allowed them to take advantage of larger stores of capital and minimize their individual risk, thereby creating an incentive to lure potential investors. Passage by the House of Commons of two bills intended to stimulate overseas trade signaled official support of the promoters' vision. Promoters, sensing their newfound acceptance, increasingly turned in their writings to the commercial benefits of trade.[52]

During the first decade of the seventeenth century, the promoters finally got what they wanted: a permanent settlement in America. In 1607, the Virginia Company, a joint-stock company set up by a group of merchants and affluent gentry, sent 144 men and boys to found a colony in the territory known as "Virginia." The settlement, which they called Jamestown, was supposed to produce crops that could be shipped to markets in England. But the management of the colony proved disastrous. Colonists kept dying, mostly because they drank water containing bacteria that caused typhoid fever and dysentery. They also suffered from malaria, salt poisoning (from drinking the water from the James River during the summer when the salt concentration was higher), and the apathy that followed malnutrition.[53] George Percy, one of the leaders of the colonization venture, described these conditions in his diary, titled "A Discourse of the Plantation of the Southern Colonie in Virginia" (see Document 6).

In response to such reports, the Virginia Company circulated accounts claiming that conditions in Jamestown were not so horrendous. One of these, *A True Declaration of the Estate of the Colonie in Virginia, with a Confutation of Such Scandalous Reports as Have Tended to the Disgrace of So Worthy an Enterprise* (see Document 7), published in London in 1610, specifically aimed to rebut any charges that the colony was failing. Remarkably, the pamphlet mentioned a colonist who killed his wife, claiming that he murdered her because he was starving and planned to eat her. In spite of such events, the Virginia Company survived into the early 1620s. Colonists in Jamestown had begun to plant tobacco in the mid-1610s and to send it to England. Since the English then demanded more and more tobacco, the settlers had an economic incentive to remain near Chesapeake Bay. And the establishment of tobacco cultivation encouraged the continued migration of thousands of English men and women for the next few decades, thereby ensuring a continued English presence on the Chesapeake. But whatever success the English might have found in tobacco production must have been tempered by the other lesson of early Virginia: America could be deadly for anyone who went there.

English ideas about American Indians crystallized during these decades. The vision of the early promoters, echoed by many others, stressed a willingness to include Indians in the life of the English colonies. To be sure, the Indians needed to change their ancestral ways, a point that, over time, colonists (especially missionaries) repeatedly stressed. The English wanted the indigenous peoples of North America to take on the cultural trappings of the English themselves. This attempt at cultural conversion went far beyond conversion to Christianity. It also entailed the replacement of indigenous languages with English, the substitution of English clothes for native dress, adoption of new settlement patterns, the institution of lifelong monogamous marriage (to replace the serial polygamy practiced by many eastern woodlands Indians), and an alteration of most traditional gender roles. Thus the promoters of colonization and their followers took it upon themselves to transform the Indians' world.

But while their goals seem, to modern eyes, hopelessly arrogant and chauvinistic, their social programs all aimed at a single result: to include Indians in civilized English society. The Indians had to be "reduced" to become civilized—that is, they had to be tamed and controlled and made less haughty—but in the end they would be, to all practical effects, English. And early promoters, especially those who actually observed Indians themselves, believed they would succeed since Indians already possessed so many of the attributes necessary for civilization: language, trade, organized society, agriculture, and a belief in a supreme being. Such attributes were not altogether surprising to these observers since Indians were, writers agreed, people whose origins ultimately lay in Genesis.[54]

THE EXPANSION OF ENGLISH COLONIZATION, 1620–1640

During the 1620s and 1630s the English expanded their settlements in North America, partly near Chesapeake Bay, where the immigrant population grew in spite of the demise of the Virginia Company in the 1620s, and also in the West Indies and New England. The settlements in New

England differed from the others in that the settlers pursued spiritual as well as economic goals. The Puritan migrants to Plymouth (founded in 1620) and Massachusetts Bay (established by charter in 1630) may have believed that moving to America would improve their material wealth, but their writings focus on the religious benefits of establishing overseas settlements.[55] For the Puritans were religious dissenters who saw in North America an escape from religious persecution and an opportunity to practice their beliefs freely (as well as to spread Protestant Christianity to the Indians).

Virtually everything the Puritans did followed from their radical Protestant beliefs. They sought to distance themselves from those who did not hold their views and criticized the Church of England, arguing that it had become corrupted through its ceremonies and open admission policies. The Puritans wanted to create new churches whose membership would be open only to individuals whom God had chosen for salvation. To include all members of the society, as the Church of England required, was an affront to God since clearly the Lord had not intended that every person be saved; mixing those destined for salvation with those destined for damnation could not be tolerated. Such beliefs had led to their persecution in England, especially during the early decades of the seventeenth century, from which some fled to New England, others to Holland (and some also remained behind).

In their many doctrinal disputes with the Church of England and among themselves, the Puritans were distinguished for their seemingly relentless effort to understand the will of an inscrutable God.[56] Their Calvinist beliefs led them to interpret every event as part of God's unfolding plan. From such a perspective, it made perfect sense that one of the leaders of Massachusetts Bay, John Winthrop, justified the migration to America in religious terms. After all, God had declared in Genesis 1:28 that people should "Increase & multiply, replenish the earth & subdue it," as Winthrop wrote in 1629 in his "Reasons to Be Considered for Justifying the Undertakers of the Intended Plantation in New England" (see Document 8). To colonize North America was, to Winthrop and other Puritans, a sacred duty. From 1630 to 1642 more than twenty thousand felt compelled to cross the ocean, flocking to New England to create Puritan communities there.

But a major problem remained: What were the Puritans supposed to do with the local Indians? On this question, the Puritans did not agree. Winthrop, for one, claimed biblical authority for seizing Indian lands since the Indians had not put them to any perceivable productive use (Winthrop and other Puritans being ignorant of the Indians' use of the land and their preservation of forests and unfenced fields).[57] Hence, Puritans presumed that English presence would improve both the land and the lives of the Indians. Besides, as Winthrop argued, God must have set the land aside for Puritans since he had "consumed the natives with a great plague" on the eve of the Puritan migration.[58]

William Bradford, the governor of Plymouth, also believed that God took the side of the English in any conflicts between the two peoples. This was clear in the Pequot War of 1637, a conflict that pitted colonists against the Pequot Indians in one of the bloodiest conflagrations of the early seventeenth century. Recalling a night when Puritans and their Narragansett allies surrounded a Pequot village on the Mystic River in what is now Connecticut, Bradford claimed that God had "wrought so wonderfully" for the Puritans when he allowed them to shoot the Indians who tried to escape the village after the Puritans set it on fire. In a world controlled by God, some Puritans believed that any and all of their actions had divine sanction.[59]

Other Puritans recognized the logistical problems with such a position and sought to take a different tack. After all, though the Puritans might have decided to leave England for religious reasons, they needed to trade with Indians in New England if they wanted to survive. Had it not been for the fur trade, the Puritan settlements of early New England might have been cut off by their London creditors. Only the supply of Indian-procured pelts enabled these colonists to pay off their debt and thus continue their efforts to create a "bible commonwealth."[60]

Some Puritans understood the importance of sharing New England with its indigenous peoples. William Wood, for one, realized that the Indians of New England were not transients who would disappear into the woods when migrants tried to establish new settlements. Wood knew that the Puritans would have to learn to coexist with their Indian neighbors. Since that was the case, he thought it best to provide potential migrants with as much information about the Indians as he could muster. His *New England's Prospect* (see Document 10), first published in 1634, thus offered his English readers more detailed information about Indian lives than did many other Puritan accounts. Wood publicized the natural resources of New England, to be sure, and informed English men and women about the status of English settlements in North America. But he took the time to describe Indian marriage patterns and Indian ideas about religion; he also wrote about the local Indians' clothing and cooking and "Of Their Dispositions and Good Qualifications, as Friendship, Constancy, Truth, and Affability." Written before the Pequot War, Wood's *Prospect* testifies to the initial English belief that Indians could be friendly trading partners instead of enemies. And he provided his readers with a glossary, a "Small

Nomenclator," of terms they would need when they spoke to Indians. To survive in New England, one had to know the local language, especially if one wanted to trade (as the Puritans did and as earlier migrants to the Chesapeake had done).[61] In the 1630s, that language was often an Algonquian dialect.

To be sure, not every promoter of overseas colonization during these years stressed the religious purpose of settlements. By the 1620s any promoter knew that the settlements near Chesapeake Bay were engaged in long-distance trade and were receiving unemployed people from England. Captain John Smith, an early leader of the Virginia Company and one of the architects of the English settlement near the Chesapeake, stressed the economic importance of trade and the need to subordinate immediate interests to the goal of building a viable commercial empire. In his writing, from his *A Description of New England* (published in 1616) to his final published work, *Advertisements for the Unexperienced Planters of New England, or Any Where, or the Path-way to Experience to Erect a Plantation* (see Document 9), printed in London in 1631, Smith emphasized the economic advantages of establishing North American colonies. Trade promised a route to wealth, Smith declared, yet it must be managed for long-term gain, not short-term profit. Smith did not abandon the religious incentive for colonization, but he did make clear that the way to success was through trade, a point that promoters echoed in ensuing decades.[62]

From 1580 to 1640, the promoters' vision of the Americas became fixed in England. Although it would be difficult to demonstrate that their ideas directly inspired the actual migration of many people, most of whom left virtually no record about what prompted them to go, more English men and women went to North America (and the West Indies) during the seventeenth century than did other Europeans. Approximately 160,000 English people went to the British mainland colonies during the seventeenth century, the vast majority (116,000) traveling to the Chesapeake region; another 190,000 migrated to the West Indies. When combined with the migration of another 180,000 to Ireland (most of them after 1640), the emigration from England to its colonies during the seventeenth century totaled more than half a million.[63] It is inconceivable that such a population transfer could have taken place without many hundreds of thousands having some idea about what life was like in the Crown's colonies, especially since some of these writings—such as those by the Hakluyts, Smith, Winthrop, and Wood—were intended specifically for would-be emigrants.

Further, the social conditions that had prompted the initial migrations remained. Over time, the rich and the poor in England found ways to accommodate one another's interests,[64] but the continuing presence of vagrants led to other plans for establishing colonies, such as Georgia, in North America. What the promoters did from the age of Elizabeth to the onset of the English Civil War in 1642 was to provide legitimation for the first wave of overseas expansion.

In 1600, Richard Hakluyt the younger wrote in the Epistle Dedicatory to the third volume of the second edition of the *Principall Navigations* that "the chiefest authors" correctly referred to America as "The New World." "New," he commented, "in regard to the new and late discovery thereof made by Christopher Colon, alias Columbus, a Genoese by nation, in the year of grace 1492. And world, in respect of the huge extension thereof, which to this day is not thoroughly discovered."[65] If the world remained undiscovered to some Europeans in 1600, it did not remain so for long, at least in part because the promoters made it so tempting for their audiences. Even tales of horror could not diminish the potential the English believed they would find across the ocean. As John Locke later put it, "[i]n the beginning all the world was America." With the promoters' ideas in mind, English migrants proceeded to conquer eastern North America and to establish themselves in what they hoped would be an earthly paradise.

NOTES

[1] Quoted in Kenneth R. Andrews, *Trade, Plunder and Settlement: Maritime Enterprise and the Genesis of the British Empire, 1480–1630* (Cambridge: Cambridge University Press, 1984), 34.

[2] James H. Merrell, " 'The Customes of Our Countrey': Indians and Colonists in Early America," in Bernard Bailyn and Philip D. Morgan, eds. *Strangers within the Realm: Cultural Margins of the First British Empire* (Chapel Hill: University of North Carolina Press, 1991), 122.

[3] The term is from Bernard Bailyn, *The Peopling of British North America: An Introduction* (New York: Alfred A. Knopf, 1986), 1–43.

[4] See Seymour Phillips, "The Medieval Background," in Nicholas Canny, ed. *Europeans on the Move* (Oxford: Oxford University Press, 1994), 9–25.

[5] Adam Smith, *An Inquiry into the Nature and Causes of the Wealth of Nations*, ed. Kathryn Sutherland (1776; Oxford: Oxford University Press, 1993), 363.

[6] Bernal Díaz del Castillo, *Historia Verdadera de la Conquista de la Nueva España*, ed. Joaquín Ramírez Cabañas, 2 vols. (Mexico: Editorial Porrua, 1955), 2:366; translated in Nancy M. Farris, *Maya Society under Colonial Rule: The Collective Enterprise of Survival* (Princeton: Princeton University Press, 1984), 29.

[7] Alfred Crosby, Jr., *The Columbian Exchange: Biological and Cultural Consequences of 1492* (Westport, Conn.: Greenwood, 1972), and *Ecological Imperialism: The Biological Expansion of Europe, 900–1900* (New York: Cambridge University Press, 1986).

[8] J. H. Parry, *The Age of Reconnaissance: Discovery, Exploration, and Settlement, 1450 to 1650* (London, 1963; reprint, Berkeley: University of California Press, 1981), 308.

[9] See "Of the Voyage for Guiana," in Robert H. Schomburgk, ed. *The Discovery of the Large, Rich, and Beautiful Empire of Guiana . . . by Sir. W. Ralegh*, Works Issued by the Hakluyt Society, no. 3 (n.d.; reprint, New York: Burt Franklin, 1970), 143.

[10] Richard Hakluyt the younger himself published a Latin version in 1587, although Richard Eden and Richard Willes had already published an English edition in 1577 (a complete version did not appear in English until 1612). For the publishing history of this work, see Francis A. MacNutt, ed. *De Orbe Novo: The Eight Decades of Peter Martyr d'Anghiera*, 2 vols. (New York: Putnam's, 1912), 1:49–52.

[11] David B. Quinn, *North America from Earliest Discovery to First Settlement: The Norse Voyages to 1612* (New York: Harper and Row, 1977), 240–61.

[12] "René de Laudonnière's views on the prospects for French overseas colonization" (1576), in David Beers Quinn and Alison O. Quinn, eds. *New American World*, 5 vols. (New York and London: Macmillan, 1979), 4:301–2.

[13] "Champlain on Motives for French Colonization in Canada," in Quinn and Quinn, *New American World*, 4:302–3.

[14] Peter Moogk, "Reluctant Exiles: Emigrants from France in Canada before 1760," *William and Mary Quarterly*, 3rd ser., 46 (1989): 463–505; Leslie Choquette, "Recruitment of French Emigrants to Canada, 1600–1760," in Ida Altman and James Horn, eds. *"To Make America": European Emigration in the Early Modern Period* (Berkeley: University of California Press, 1991), 137, 158–61.

[15] For documents relating to Hudson's voyage, see Quinn and Quinn, *New American World*, 3:467–91. For an excellent analysis of Dutch migrations during the early modern period, see Jan Lucassen, "The Netherlands, the Dutch, and Long-Distance Migration in the Late Sixteenth to Early Nineteenth Centuries," in Canny, *Europeans on the Move*, 153–91.

[16] Karen Ordahl Kupperman, *Roanoke: The Abandoned Colony* (Savage, Md.: Rowman and Littlefield, 1984), 102–3.

[17] For the earliest English voyages, see David Beers Quinn, *England and the Discovery of America, 1481–1620* (London: Allen and Unwin, 1974), 5–23. The English were not the first Europeans to see the Canadian maritime provinces: the Norse had traveled to North America almost five centuries before Columbus; see Crosby, *Ecological Imperialism*, 44–56. For an excellent treatment of Bristol and the Atlantic, see David Harris Sacks, *The Widening Gate: Bristol and the Atlantic Economy, 1450–1700* (Berkeley: University of California Press, 1991).

[18] Thomas More, *The Best State of a Commonwealth and the New Island of Utopia* (1516), in Edward Surtz and J. H. Hexter, eds., *The Complete Works of St. Thomas More* (New Haven: Yale University Press, 1965), 4:137; see also Nicholas Canny, "Theories of Colonization and Some of Their Applications" (paper presented at the Harvard University Early Modern Cultural Crossings Seminar, April 1992), 1–12.

[19] Sir William Herbert, *Croftus Sive de Hibernia Liber*, ed. Arthur Keaveny and John A. Madden (Dublin: Irish Manuscripts Commission, 1992), 81.

[20] On these early efforts, see R. R. Davies, *Domination and Conquest: The Experience of Ireland, Scotland, and Wales, 1100–1300* (Cambridge: Cambridge University Press, 1990).

[21] Nicholas P. Canny, "The Ideology of English Colonization: From Ireland to America," *William and Mary Quarterly*, 3rd ser., 30 (1973), 575–98. Canny describes the conflict in greater depth in his *The Elizabethan Conquest of Ireland: A Pattern Established, 1565–76* (Hassocks, Sussex: Harvester Press, 1976).

[22] Michael McCarthy Morrogh, "The English Presence in Early Seventeenth Century Munster," in Ciaran Brady and Raymond Gillespie, eds. *Natives and Newcomers: Essays on the Making of Irish Colonial Society, 1534–1641* (Bungay, Suffolk: Irish Academic Press, 1986), 171–90; Nicholas Canny, "The 1641 Depositions as a Source for the Writing of Social History: County Cork as a Case Study," in Patrick O'Flanagan and Cornelius B. Buttimer, eds. *Cork History and Society: Interdisciplinary Essays on the History of an Irish County* (Dublin: Geography Publications, 1993), 249–308; Nicholas Canny, "The Irish Background to Penn's Experiment," in Richard S. Dunn and Mary Maples Dunn, eds. *The World of*

William Penn (Philadelphia: University of Pennsylvania Press, 1986), 139–56. Elsewhere in Ireland the migration of large numbers of Scots made the situation even more complex, though again not necessarily violent; see Nicholas Canny, "The Marginal Kingdom: Ireland as a Problem in the First British Empire," in Bailyn and Morgan, *Strangers within the Realm,* 48–53.

[23] E. A. Wrigley and R. S. Schofield, *The Population History of England, 1541–1871* (Cambridge: Harvard University Press, 1981), 531–32.

[24] For changes in the economy, particularly the erosion of long-standing practices, see Joyce Appleby, *Economic Thought and Ideology in Seventeenth-Century England* (Princeton: Princeton University Press, 1978), 28, 54–55, 59; for migrations from England to the Chesapeake, see James P. P. Horn, "Servant Emigration to the Chesapeake in the Seventeenth Century," in Thad Tate and David Ammerman, eds. *The Chesapeake in the Seventeenth Century* (Chapel Hill: University of North Carolina Press, 1979), 51–95. Migrations did not end for many Britons when they arrived in America; many continued to move, again seeking better opportunity. See James P. P. Horn, "Moving on in the New World: Migration and Out-Migration in the Seventeenth-Century Chesapeake," in Peter Clark and David Souden, eds. *Migration and Society in Early Modern England* (London: Hutchinson, 1987), 192–212.

[25] See Georg Fertig, "Transatlantic Migration from the German-Speaking Parts of Central Europe, 1600–1800: Proportions, Structures and Explanations," and Nicholas Canny, "In Search of a Better Home? European Overseas Migration, 1500–1800," in Canny, *Europeans on the Move,* 192–235, 263–83.

[26] A. L. Beier, *Masterless Men: The Vagrancy Problem in England, 1560–1640* (London: Methuen, 1985), esp. 4, 8, 56, 69, 73, 85.

[27] Joyce Youings, *Sixteenth-Century England* (Harmondsworth, England: Penguin, 1984), 254–59; Beier, *Masterless Men,* 4–5.

[28] Beier, *Masterless Men,* 40; Paul Slack, *Poverty and Policy in Tudor and Stuart England* (London: Longman, 1988), 69–71.

[29] Beier, *Masterless Men,* 164–69.

[30] Sebastian Cabot to Charles V, November 15, 1553, in Joyce Lorimer, ed. *English and Irish Settlement on the River Amazon, 1550–1646,* Works Issued by the Hakluyt Society, 2nd ser., no. 171 (1989), 127–28.

[31] Appleby, *Economic Thought and Ideology,* 73–98, esp. 96–98. For a splendid analysis of Dutch wealth, with a special focus on the seventeenth century, see Simon Schama, *The Embarrassment of Riches: An Interpretation of Dutch Culture in the Golden Age* (New York: Alfred A. Knopf, 1987), esp. 290–323.

[32] Entrepreneurs during this age used whatever political power they could muster to shape the Crown's economic policies; to do so, they sought powerful patrons. For the expansion of trade and its social context, see Robert Brenner, "The Social Basis of English Commercial Expansion, 1550–1650," *Journal of Economic History* 32 (1972): 361–84, esp. 362–74, and Karen Ordahl Kupperman, *Settling with the Indians: The Meeting of English and Indian Cultures in America, 1580–1640* (Totowa, N.J.: Rowman and Littlefield, 1980), 9.

[33] Quoted in Beier, *Masterless Men,* 150.

[34] Carole Shammas, "English Commercial Development and American Colonization, 1560–1620," in K. R. Andrews, N. P. Canny, and P. E. H. Hair, eds. *The Westward Enterprise: English Activities in Ireland, the Atlantic, and America, 1480–1650* (Liverpool: Liverpool University Press, 1978), 158–59, 163–64; Kupperman, *Settling with the Indians,* 248.

[35] Richard Hakluyt (the younger), *Divers Voyages Touching the Discovery of America and the Ilands Adjacent* (1582), Works Issued by the Hakluyt Society, 1st ser., no. 7 (London, [1850]; reprint, New York, n.d.), 8–9, 16.

[36] Richard Hakluyt (the younger), *"Discourse of Western Planting"* (1584), in E. G. R. Taylor, ed. *The Original Writings and Correspondence of the Two Richard Hakluyts,* Works Issued for the Hakluyt Society, 2nd ser. (London, 1935), 77:234–35, 76:33–39. By the early seventeenth century many of those who promulgated works involving the employment of the

indigent had been linked to corruption at the heart of the empire; Daniel Defoe wrote that "projector" was a "despicable title." But in Elizabethan England, as Joan Thirsk has demonstrated, such projects were vital to boost the economy of poor areas and stimulated the emergence of a consumer society. See Thirsk's *Economic Policy and Projects: The Development of a Consumer Society in Early Modern England* (Oxford, England: Clarendon, 1978); the quotation from Defoe is on pages 17–18. For one example of the potential success of projects in Elizabethan England, see Thirsk, "Projects for Gentlemen, Jobs for the Poor: Mutual Aid in the Vale of Tewksbury, 1600–1630," in Thirsk, *The Rural Economy of England: Collected Essays* (London: Hambledon, 1984), 287–307.

[37] Kenneth R. Andrews, *Trade, Plunder, and Settlement*, 10–11.

[38] Originally in Hakluyt, *Principall Navigations* (1589); reprinted as "A New Land like unto That of the Golden Age (1584–85)," in Louis B. Wright, ed. *The Elizabethans' America* (Cambridge: Harvard University Press, 1966), 109.

[39] The best overview of the venture is Kupperman, *Roanoke*.

[40] Kupperman, *Roanoke*, 17.

[41] Quinn, *North America*, 551.

[42] For one collection of images, see Susi Colin, "The Wild Man and the Indian in Early 16th Century Book Illustration," in Christian F. Feest, ed. *Indians and Europe: An Interdisciplinary Collection of Essays* (Aachen, Germany: Edition Herodot, 1987), 5–36. On English perceptions of Africans, see Winthrop D. Jordan, *White over Black: American Attitudes toward the Negro, 1550–1812* (Chapel Hill: University of North Carolina Press, 1968), esp. chap. 1.

[43] Thomas Harriot, "A briefe and true report of the new found land of Virginia," in Quinn and Quinn, *New American World*, 3:151. For the importance of his native informants, see Kupperman, *Roanoke*, 16 ff.

[44] See Paul Hulton, introduction to Thomas Harriot, *A Briefe and True Report of the New Found Land of Virginia* (New York: Dover, 1972), xi.

[45] Paul Hulton, *America 1585: The Complete Drawings of John White* (Chapel Hill: University of North Carolina Press, 1984); the quotation appears on page 130. Picts captured the imagination of antiquarians in early modern England; see Stuart Piggott, *Ancient Britons and the Antiquarian Imagination: Ideas from the Renaissance to the Regency* (London: Thames and Hudson, 1989), esp. 76–85.

[46] As Karen Ordahl Kupperman has pointed out, even perceptions of Indians' treachery could be a sign of their potential for civilization: "In fact, far from being peculiar to savagery, treachery in these [early modern English] writings is regarded as a mark of competence, even of civilization. The fact that the Indians were treacherous meant that the English must respect them; they were worthy opponents." See Kupperman, "English Perceptions of Treachery, 1583–1640: The Case of the American 'Savages,' " *Historical Journal* 20 (1977): 286–87. Other writers too stressed the potential for converting Indians to European ways; see, among other works, [Robert Johnson], *Nova Britannia offering most Excellent Fruites by Planting in Virginia* (London, 1609), in Quinn and Quinn, *New American World*, 5:234–48; [Robert Johnson], *The New Life of Virginia, Declaring the Former Success and Present Estate of That Plantation, Being the Second Part of Nova Britannia* (London, 1612; reprint, Rochester, 1897–1898), pamphlet 7, William Strachey, *The Histories of Travell into Virginia Britannia* (1612), ed. Louis B. Wright and Virginia Freund, Works Issued by the Hakluyt Society, 2nd ser., 103 (Lonon, 1953), 89:24–25, 54–55; and Alexander Whitaker, *Good Newes from Virginia* (London, 1613; reprint, New York, n.d.), 33, 40.

[47] Kupperman, *Roanoke*, 11, 147–50, 155–58.

[48] Richard Hakluyt, *Voyages and Discoveries: The Principal Navigations, Voyages, Traffiques and Discoveries of the English Nation*, ed. Jack Beeching (London: Penguin, 1985), 27.

[49] George Peckham, "A True Report of the Late Discoveries . . . of the New Found

Lands . . . by Sir Humphrey Gilbert," in Richard Hakluyt, *Principall Voyages,* 8 vols. (London: Modern Library, 1907), 6:52–54.

[50] Richard Hakluyt, "Epistle Dedicatorie in the First Edition, 1589," in Hakluyt, *Principall Voyages,* 1:1. Ralegh too used scriptural justifications for his actions; see "Of the Voyage for Guiana," esp. 141–46.

[51] The Puritans had no monopoly on the use of biblical justifications in later decades; see, for example, the logic of the transplanted Scot William Alexander, who wanted to establish a colony in Nova Scotia, in *An Encouragement to Colonies* (London, 1624), 1–2. Captain John Smith also drew on the Bible for inspiration; see his *Advertisements for the Unexperienced Planters of New England, or Any Where, or the Path-Way to Experience to Erect a Plantation* (London, 1631), in Philip L. Barbour, ed. *The Complete Works of Captain John Smith,* 3 vols. (Chapel Hill: University of North Carolina Press, 1986), 3:276–77. For the importance of religion to Smith, see Nicholas Canny, " 'To Establish a Common Wealthe': Captain John Smith as New World Colonist," *Virginia Magazine of History and Biography* 96 (1988): 213–22. Other writers too noted biblical parallels, especially the migration of the Israelites to Canaan, in their promotional writings; see Kupperman, *Settling with the Indians,* 166–67.

[52] Shammas, "English Commercial Development," 163–67.

[53] On the suffering of colonists in early Jamestown, see Carville Earle, "Environment, Disease, and Mortality in Early Virginia," in Tate and Ammerman, *Chesapeake,* 96–125, and Karen Ordahl Kupperman, "Apathy and Death in Early Jamestown," *Journal of American History* 66 (1979): 24–40.

[54] On the entire cultural program of the English, see James Axtell, "The Invasion Within: The Contest of Cultures in Colonial North America," in Axtell, *The European and the Indian: Essays in the Ethnohistory of Colonial North America* (New York: Oxford University Press, 1981), 39–86. On early observers' beliefs about the necessary preconditions for cultural conversion and the importance of eyewitness accounts, see Kupperman, *Settling with the Indians,* 47, 56–57, 62–63, 70, 108, 112–113, 160.

[55] See Virginia DeJohn Anderson, "Migrants and Motives: Religion and the Settlement of New England, 1630–1640," *New England Quarterly* 58 (1985): 339–83.

[56] Still one of the best overviews of Puritan thought is Edmund Morgan, *Visible Saints: The History of a Puritan Idea* (1963; reprint, Ithaca, N.Y.: Cornell University Press, 1965).

[57] See William Cronon, *Changes in the Land: Indians, Colonists, and the Ecology of New England* (New York: Hill and Wang, 1983).

[58] John Winthrop, "Reasons to be Considered . . . ," in Alan Heimert and Andrew Delbanco, eds. *The Puritans in America: A Narrative Anthology* (Cambridge: Harvard University Press, 1985), 73.

[59] William Bradford, *Of Plymouth Plantation,* ed. Samuel Eliot Morison (1952; reprint, New York: Modern Library, 1967), 296.

[60] Though Bradford might not have agreed with this assessment, his own history of Plymouth reveals the importance of the fur trade to the colony's survival; see Bradford, *Of Plymouth Plantation.*

[61] For New England, see Neal Salisbury, *Manitou and Providence: Indians, Europeans, and the Making of New England, 1500–1643* (New York: Oxford University Press, 1982); for the Chesapeake, see Edmund Morgan, *American Slavery, American Freedom: The Ordeal of Colonial Virginia* (New York: Norton, 1975), esp. chap. 4; for trading food after the hostilities of 1622, see Kupperman, *Settling with the Indians,* 182; for the origins of trade, see James Axtell, "At the Water's Edge: Trading in the Sixteenth Century," in Axtell, *After Columbus: Essays in the Ethnohistory of Colonial North America* (New York: Oxford University Press, 1988), 144–81.

[62] Shammas, "English Commercial Development," 173–74. For one particularly good example from the 1630s, see Lewes Roberts, *The Merchants Mapp of Commerce* (London, 1638), esp. 42–44; for an excellent example from the late seventeenth century, see Samuel Clarke, *A Geographical Description of All the Countries in the Known World* (London, 1671).

[63] Nicholas Canny, "English Migration into and across the Atlantic during the Seventeenth and Eighteenth Centuries," in Canny, *Europeans on the Move,* 64.

[64] As E. P. Thompson has demonstrated, the poor remained a threat to the social order well beyond the seventeenth century, but their limited outbursts did not undermine the larger economy of the society; see "The Moral Economy of the English Crowd in the Eighteenth Century," *Past and Present* 50 (1971): 76–136.

[65] Hakluyt, *Principall Voyages,* 1:47.

PART TWO

The Documents

1

RICHARD HAKLUYT (THE ELDER)

"Inducements to the Liking of the Voyage Intended towards Virginia in 40. and 42. Degrees"

1585

Richard Hakluyt the elder was a prominent lawyer who became interested in overseas colonization in the 1570s. According to his cousin Richard Hakluyt the younger (author of the "Discourse of Western Planting," Document 2), the elder Hakluyt had first nourished the younger's interest in explorations by pointing "with his wand" at a "universal Map" that showed the known places of the world in the mid-sixteenth century. The elder Hakluyt replayed that rhetorical gesture in more important ways by setting down in print his views on the possibilities of expanding English settlements across the Atlantic. "Inducements," written in 1585, serves as testimony to the initial British interest in North America.

In "Inducements" Hakluyt provided a list of justifications for colonization and an itemization of the goods to be obtained or cultivated in North America. Hakluyt stressed, as many other promoters did, the religious benefits of colonization as well as the political: to enlarge not only "the force of the Christians" but also the dominion of Queen Elizabeth I. Hakluyt then moved on to the practical concerns of a seafaring nation, noting the strategic and economic advantages of establishing settlements in America.

Significantly, Hakluyt's "Inducements" acknowledged the role of Indians in any colonization scheme. For settlements to survive, it would be best, he argued, to establish peaceful relations with America's natives; "trafficke easily followeth conquest," he declared, adding that Indians would also benefit from commerce. Hakluyt was uneasy about hostilities that might emerge between colonists and natives; he noted at one point that their superiority in navigation gave the English a great advantage over any troublesome Indians, but he stressed later that any overly vengeful acts by the English would lead to disaster.

Richard Hakluyt (the elder), "Inducements to the Liking of the Voyage Intended towards Virginia in 40. and 42. Degrees," in David Beers Quinn and Alison O. Quinn, eds. *New American World*, 5 vols. (New York and London: Macmillan, 1979), 3:64–69.

Hakluyt was more certain of the ways that colonization could improve England's domestic situation, in particular the problem of the poor. Transplanted overseas, unemployed youths who threatened the social order could be put to work producing goods valued in Britain. Hakluyt's list of the types of migrants who would best populate and develop colonies testified to this belief, though he never made clear how the unemployed, and presumably unskilled, of England would gain the skills necessary for prosperity in America.

Hakluyt's plan now seems misguided, especially his enthusiasm for the types of commodities that could be found or cultivated in eastern North America. But since it was written more than two decades before the founding of the first permanent English settlement at Jamestown, and three years before the English would gain unfettered access to the sea by defeating the Spanish Armada, his miscalculations are certainly understandable. What were some of Hakluyt's miscalculations? What do his errors reveal about the earliest English goals in colonizing North America? How might the expectations of would-be immigrants to North America have been shaped by Hakluyt's "Inducements"? Why do you think Hakluyt placed religion first in his list of three "ends of this voyage" (p. 39) and first in his list of "Inducements" (below)? What does his enumeration of the types of workers for the colony reveal about the plans of the promoters of colonization?

1. The glory of God by planting of religion among those infidels.

2. The increase of the force of the Christians.

3. The possibilitie of the inlarging of the dominions of the Queenes most excellent Majestie, and consequently of her honour, revenues, and of her power by this enterprise.

4. An ample vent[1] in time to come of the Woollen clothes of England, especially those of the coursest sorts, to the maintenance of our poore, that els sterve or become burdensome to the realme: and vent also of sundry our commodities upon the tract of that firme land, and possibly in other regions from the Northerne side of that maine.[2]

5. A great possibilitie of further discoveries of other regions from the North part of the same land by sea, and of unspeakable honor and benefit that may rise upon the same, by the trades to ensue in Japan, China, and Cathay,[3] &c.

6. By returne thence, this realme shall receive (by reason of the situation of the climate, and by reason of the excellent soile) Oade,[4] Oile,

---

[1] Market.
[2] Mainland.
[3] Northern China.
[4] Oade is woad, a blue dye-stuff produced from powdered and fermented leaves of *Isatis tinctoria*, a plant sometimes called garden woad or dyer's weed.

Wines, Hops, Salt, and most or all the commodities that we receive from the best parts of Europe, and we shall receive the same better cheape, than now we receive them, as we may use the matter.

7. Receiving the same thence, the navie, the humane strength of this realme, our merchants and their goods shal not be subject to arrest of ancient enemies & doubtfull friends, as of late yeeres they have beene.

8. If our nation do not make any conquest there, but only use trafficke and change of commodities, yet by meane the countrey is not very mightie, but divided into pety kingdoms, they shall not dare to offer us any great annoy, but such as we may easily revenge with sufficient chastisement to the unarmed people there.

9. Whatsoever commodities we receive by the Steelyard merchants, or by our owne merchants from Eastland,[5] be it Flaxe, Hempe, Pitch, Tarre, Masts, Clap-boord,[6] Wainscot,[7] or such like; the like good may we receive from the North and Northeast part of that countrey neere unto Cape Briton,[8] in returne for our course Woollen clothes, Flanels and Rugges fit for those colder regions.

10. The passage to and fro, is thorow the maine Ocean sea, so as we are not in danger of any enemies coast.

11. In the voyage, we are not to crosse the burnt Zone,[9] nor to passe thorow frozen seas encombred with ice and fogs, but in temperate climate at all times of the yeere: and it requireth not, as the East Indie voiage doth, the taking in of water in divers places, by reason that it is to be sailed in five or six weeks: and by the shortnesse, the merchant may yeerely make two returnes (a factory once being erected there) a matter in trade of great moment.[10]

12. In this trade by the way in our passe to and fro, we have in tempests and other haps, all the ports of Ireland to our aid, and no neere coast of any enemy.

13. By this ordinary trade we may annoy the enemies to Ireland, and succour the Queenes Majesties friends there, and in time we may from Virginia yeeld them whatsoever commoditie they now receive from the Spaniard; and so the Spaniards shall want the ordinary victual[11] that heertofore they received yeerely from thence, and so they shall not

---

[5] The lands bordering on the Baltic Sea.

[6] A narrow board of split oak, imported into England from northern Germany and used for making barrel staves.

[7] A superior quality of foreign oak imported into England from Russia, Germany, and Holland and chiefly used for fine paneling.

[8] Island east of present-day Nova Scotia.

[9] Tropics.

[10] Of great importance.

[11] Food or provisions.

continue trade, nor fall so aptly in practise against this government, as now by their trade thither[12] they may.

14. We shall, as it is thought, enjoy in this voyage, either some small Islands to settle on, or some one place or other on the firme land to fortifie for the saftie of our ships, our men, and our goods, the like whereof we have not in any forren place of our trafficke,[13] in which respect we may be in degree of more safetie, and more quiet.

15. The great plentie of Buffe[14] hides, and of many other sundry kinds of hides there now presently to be had, the trade of Whale and Seale fishing, and of divers other fishings in the great rivers, great bayes, and seas there, shall presently defray the charge in good part or in all of the first enterprise, and so we shall be in better case than our men were in Russia, where many yeeres were spent, and great summes of money consumed, before gaine was found.

16. The great broad rivers of that maine that we are to enter into so many leagues navigable or portable into the maine land, lying so long a tract with so excellent and so fertile a soile on both sides, doe seeme to promise all things that the life of man doth require, and whatsoever men may wish, that are to plant upon the same, or to trafficke in the same.

17. And whatsoever notable commoditie the soile within or without doth yeeld in so long a tract that is to be carried out from thence to England, the same rivers so great and deepe, do yeeld no small benefit for the sure, safe, easie and cheape cariage of the same to shipboord, be it of great bulke or of great weight.

18. And in like sort whatsoever commoditie of England the Inland people there shall need, the same rivers doe worke the like effect in benefit for the incariage of the same, aptly, easily, and cheaply.

19. If we finde the countrey populous, and desirous to expel us, and injuriously to offend us, that seeke but just and lawful trafficke, then by reason that we are lords of navigation, and they not so, we are the better able to defend our selves by reason of those great rivers, & to annoy them in many places.

20. Where there be many petie kings or lords planted on the rivers sides, and by all likelihood mainteine the frontiers of their severall territories by warres, we may by the aide of this river joine with this king heere, or with that king there, at our pleasure, and may so with a few men be revenged of any wrong offered by any of them; or may, if we will proceed

---

[12] Until then.
[13] Trade or commerce.
[14] Buffalo or other large species of wild ox.

with extremitie,[15] conquer, fortifie, and plant in soiles most sweet, most pleasant, most strong, and most fertile, and in the end bring them all in subjection and to civilitie.

21. The knowen abundance of Fresh fish in the rivers, and the knowen plentie of Fish on the sea coast there, may assure us of sufficient victuall in spight of the people, if we will use salt and industrie.

22. The knowen plentie and varietie of Flesh, of divers kinds of beasts at land there, may seeme to say to us, that we may cheaply victuall our navies to England for our returnes, which benefit every where is not found of merchants.

23. The practise of the people of the East Indies, when the Portugals came thither first, was to cut from the Portugals their lading of Spice: and heereby they thought to overthrow their purposed trade. If these people shall practise the like, by not suffering[16] us to have any commoditie of theirs without conquest, (which requireth some time) yet may we mainteine our first voyage thither, till our purpose come to effect, by the sea-fishing on the coasts there, and by dragging for pearles, which are said to be on those parts; and by returne of those commodities, the charges in part shall be defraied: which is a matter of consideration in enterprises of charge.

24. If this realme shall abound too too much with youth, in the mines there of Golde, (as that of Chisca and Saguenay)[17] of Silver, Copper, Yron, &c. may be an imployment to the benefit of this realme; in tilling of the rich soile there for graine, and in planting of Vines there for Wine; or dressing of those Vines which grow there naturally in great abundance, Olives for Oile; Orenge trees, Limons, Figs and Almonds for fruit; Oad, Saffron, and Madder[18] for Diers; Hoppes for Brewers; Hempe, Flaxe; and in many such other things, by imploiment of the soile, our people void of sufficient trades, may be honestly imploied, that els may become hurtfull at home.

25. The navigating of the seas in the voyage, and of the great rivers there, will breed many Mariners for service, and mainteine much navigation.

26. The number of raw Hides there of divers kindes of beasts, if we shall possesse some Island there, or settle on the firme, may presently imploy many of our idle people in divers severall dressings of the same, and so we may returne them to the people that can not dresse them so well; or into this realm, where the same are good merchandize; or to

---

[15] Extreme intensity or violence.

[16] Allowing, giving permission, tolerating.

[17] The Saguenay is a river in northeastern Canada flowing into the St. Lawrence River.

[18] A herbaceous climbing plant cultivated for the dye obtained from it.

Flanders,[19] &c. which present gaine at the first, raiseth great incourage-
ment presently to the enterprise.

27. Since great waste Woods be there, of Oake, Cedar, Pine, Wall-
nuts, and sundry other sorts, many of our waste people may be imployed
in making of Ships, Hoies, Busses[20] and Boats; and in making of Rozen,
Pitch and Tarre, the trees naturall for the same, being certeinly knowen to
be neere Cape Briton and the Bay of Menan,[21] and in many other places
there about.

28. If mines of white or gray marble, Jet, or other rich stone be found
there, our idle people may be imployed in the mines of the same, and in
preparing the same to shape, and so shaped, they may be caried into this
realm as good balast[22] for our ships, and after serve for noble buildings.

29. Sugar-canes may be planted as well as they are now in the South of
Spaine, and besides the imploiment of our idle people, we may receive the
commodity cheaper, and not inrich infidels or our doubtful friends, of
whom now we receive that commoditie.

30. The daily great increase of Woolles in Spaine, and the like in the
West Indies, and the great imploiment of the same into Cloth in both
places, may moove us to endevour, for vent of our Cloth, new discoveries
of peopled regions, where hope of sale may arise; otherwise in short time
many inconveniences may possibly ensue.

31. This land that we purpose to direct our course to, lying in part in
the 40 degree of latitude, being in like heat as Lisbone in Portugall doth,
and in the more Southerly part as the most Southerly coast of Spaine doth,
may by our diligence yeeld unto us besides Wines and Oiles and Sugars,
Orenges, Limons, Figs, Resings,[23] Almonds, Pomegranates, Rice, Raw-
silks such as come from Granada, and divers commodities for Diers, as
Anile and Cochenillio,[24] and sundry other colours and materials. Moreover, we shall not onely receive many precious commodities besides from
thence, but also shal in time finde ample vent of the labour of our poore
people at home, by sale of Hats, Bonets, Knives, Fish-hooks, Copper
kettles, Beads, Looking-glasses, Bugles, & a thousand kinds of other
wrought wares, that in short time may be brought in use among the people

---

[19] Present-day Belgium.

[20] Hoys were small boats often used to carry people and goods along the coast. Busses
were two- or three-masted fishing boats.

[21] Perhaps present-day Grand Manan Channel, off the southwest coast of New Bruns-
wick, Canada.

[22] Ballast, heavy material placed in the hold of a ship to prevent capsizing when in motion.

[23] Raisins.

[24] Anil is the indigo shrub or dye. Cochineal is a dyestuff consisting of the dried bodies of
Coccus cacti, an insect found on several species of cactus; it produces a brilliant scarlet dye.

of that countrey, to the great reliefe of the multitude of our poore people, and to the woonderfull enriching of this realme. And in time, such league & entercourse may arise betweene our Stapling[25] seats there, and other ports of our Northern America, and of the Islands of the same, that incredible things, and by few as yet dreamed of, may speedily follow, tending to the impeachment of our mightie enemies, and to the common good of this noble government.

The ends of this voyage are these:

1. To plant Christian religion.
2. To trafficke.[26]
3. To conquer.

Or, to doe all three.

To plant Christian religion without conquest, will bee hard. Trafficke easily followeth conquest: conquest is not easie. Trafficke without conquest seemeth possible, and not uneasie. What is to be done, is the question.

If the people be content to live naked, and to content themselves with few things of meere necessity, then trafficke is not. So then in vaine seemeth our voyage, unlesse this nature may be altered, as by conquest and other good meanes it may be, but not on a sudden. The like whereof appeared in the East Indies, upon the Portugals seating there.

If the people in the Inland be clothed, and desire to live in the abundance of all such things as Europe doth, and have at home all the same in plentie, yet we can not have trafficke with them, by meane they want not any thing that we can yeeld them.

Admit that they have desire to your commodities, and as yet have neither Golde, Silver, Copper, Iron, nor sufficient quantitie of other present commoditie to mainteine the yeerely trade: What is then to be done?

The soile and climate first is to be considered, and you are with Argus eies[27] to see what commoditie by industrie of man you are able to make it to yeeld, that England doth want or doth desire: as for the purpose, if you can make it to yeeld good Wine, or good Oile, as it is like you may by the climat, (where wilde Vines of sundry sorts doe naturally grow already in great abundance) then your trade may be mainteined. But admit the soile

---

[25] Referring to a town or place, appointed by royal authority, where a group of merchants had exclusive rights to buy and export commodities.

[26] To carry on trade.

[27] Like a watcher or guardian, after Argus, a mythological person fabled to have had a hundred eyes.

were in our disposition (as yet it is not) in what time may this be brought about?

For Wine this is to be affirmed, that first the soile lying in 36 or 37 degrees in the temperature of South Spaine, in setting your Vine-plants this yeere, you may have Wine within three yeeres. And it may be that the wilde Vines growing there already, by orderly pruning and dressing at your first arrivall, may come to profit in shorter time.

And planting your Olive trees this yeere, you may have Oile within three yeeres.

And if the sea shores be flat, and fit for receipt of salt water, and for Salt making, without any annoy of neere freshes,[28] then the trade of Salt onely may mainteine a yeerely navigation (as our men now trade to the isle of Maio,[29] and the Hollanders to Terra Firma neere the West end of the isle of Margarita.)[30]

But how the naturall people of the countrey may be made skilfull to plant Vines, and to know the use, or to set Olive trees, and to know the making of Oile, and withall to use both the trades, that is a matter of small consideration: but to conquer a countrey or province in climate & soile of Italie, Spaine, or the Islands from whence we receive our Wines & Oiles, and to man it, to plant it, and to keepe it, and to continue the making of Wines and Oiles able to serve England, were a matter of great importance both in respect of the saving at home of our great treasure now yeerely going away, and in respect of the annoyance thereby growing to our enemies. The like consideration would be had, touching a place for the making of Salt, of temperature like those of France, not too colde, as the Salts of the Northern regions be; nor too too firy, as those be that be made more Southerly than France. In regard whereof, many circumstances are to be considered; and principally, by what meane the people of those parties may be drawen by all courtesie into love with our nation; that we become not hatefull unto them, as the Spaniard is in Italie and in the West Indies, and elswhere, by their maner of usage: for a gentle course without crueltie and tyrannie best answereth the profession of a Christian, best planteth Christian religion; maketh our seating most void of blood, most profitable in trade of merchandise, most firme and stable, and least subject to remoove by practise of enemies. But that we may in seating there, not be subject wholly to the malice of enemies, and may be more able to preserve our bodies, ships, and goods in more safetie, and

---

[28] Runoff of fresh (river) water.
[29] One of the Cape Verde Islands off the western coast of Africa.
[30] The "Isle of Pearls," in the Caribbean off the coast of Venezuela.

to be knowen to be more able to scourge[31] the people there, civill or savage, than willing to offer any violence. And for the more quiet exercise of our manurance[32] of the soiles where we shall seat, and of our manuall occupations, it is to be wished that some ancient captaines of milde disposition and great judgement be sent thither with men most skilfull in the arte of fortification; and that direction be taken that the mouthes of great rivers, and the Islands in the same (as things of great moment) be taken, manned, and fortified; and that havens be cut out for safetie of the Navie, that we may be lords of the gates and entries, to goe out and come in at pleasure, and to lie in safetie, and be able to command and to controle all within, and to force all forren navigation to lie out in open rode subject to all weathers, to be dispersed by tempests and flawes, if the force within be not able to give them the encounter abroad.

1. The Red Muscadell grape, that bishop Grindall procured out of Germanie; the great White Muscadell; the Yellow grape: the cuts of these were woont yeerely to be set at Fulham; and after one yeeres rooting to be given by the bishop, and to be sold by his gardener. These presently provided, and placed in earth, and many of these so rooted, with store of cuts unrooted besides, placed in tubbes of earth shipped at the next voyage, to be planted in Virginia, may begin Vineyards, and bring Wines out of hand.

2. Provision great of wilde Olive trees may be made out of this citie so then to be caried, to encrease great store of stocks to graffe the best Olive on: and Virginia standing in the same degree that The Shroffe[33] the Olive place doth in Spaine, we may win that merchandise, graffing the wilde.[34]

3. Sugar-canes, if you can not procure them from the Spanish Islands, yet may you by your Barberie[35] merchants procure them.

4. There is an herbe in Persia, whereof Anile is made, and it is also in Barbarie: to procure that by seed or root, were of importance for a trade of merchandise for our clothing countrey.

5. Oad by the seeds you may have; for you may have hundreds of bushels in England, as it is multiplied: and having soile and labor in Virginia cheape, and the Oad in great value, lying in small roome, it will be a trade of great gaine to this clothing realme: and the thing can not be destroyed

[31] Punish, chastise, or correct.
[32] Control or occupation.
[33] Presumably a garbled version of a place in southern Spain where olives were grown.
[34] Grafting wild (presumably American) olive trees with cultivated (European) trees.
[35] Barbary is a region in North Africa extending from the west of Egypt to the Atlantic Ocean.

by Salvages.[36] The roots of this you may have in plenty and number comming in the trade: so this may grow in trade within a yeere ready for the merchant.

6. Figge trees of many good kinds may be had hence in barrell, if now presently they be provided; and they in that climat will yeeld noble fruit, and feed your people presently, and will be brought in frailes[37] home as merchandise, or in barrell, as Resings also may be.

7. Sawed boords of Sassafras and Cedar, to be turned into small boxes for ladies and gentlewomen, would become a present trade.

8. To the infinite naturall increase of Hogs, to adde a device how the same may be fed by roots, acornes, &c. without spoiling your corne, would be of great effect to feed the multitude continually imployed in labour: and the same cheaply bred and salted, and barrelled there and brought home, will be well solde for a good merchandise; and the barrels after, will serve for our home Herring-fishing; and so you sell your woods and the labour of your cooper.[38]

9. Receiving the salvage women and their children of both sexes by courtesie into your protection, and imploying the English women and the others in making of Linnen, you shal raise a woonderfull trade of benefit, both to carie into England and also into the Islands, and into the maine of the West Indies, victuall and labour being so cheape there.

10. The trade of making cables and cordage there, will be of great importance, in respect of a cheape maintenance of the Navie that shall passe to and fro; and in respect of such Navie as may in those parties be used for the venting of the commodities of England to be brought thither. And Powldavies,[39] &c. made for sailes of the poore Salvages, yeeld to the Navie a great helpe, and a great gaine in the trafficke.

But if seeking revenge on every injurie of the Salvages we seeke blood & raise war, our Vines, our Olives, our Figge trees, our Sugar-canes, our Orenges and Limons, Corne, Cattell, &c. will be destroyed, and trade of merchandise in all things overthrowen; and so the English nation there planted and to be planted, shall be rooted out with sword and hunger.

Sorts of men which are to be passed in this voyage

1. Men skilfull in all Minerall causes.[40]
2. Men skilfull in all kinde of drugges.

---

[36] Savages; i.e., Indians.
[37] Basket made of rushes, used for packing raisins or figs.
[38] Someone who makes and repairs barrels.
[39] Poldavy was a coarse canvas used for sailcloth.
[40] Mining.

3. Fishermen, to consider of the sea fishings there on the coasts, to be reduced to trade hereafter: and others for the fresh water fishings.

4. Salt-makers, to view the coast, and to make triall how rich the sea-water there is, to advise for the trade.

5. Husbandmen,[41] to view the soile, to resolve for tillage in all sorts.

6. Vineyard-men bred, to see how the soile may serve for the planting of Vines.

7. Men bred in the Shroffe in South Spaine, for discerning how Olive trees may be planted there.

8. Others, for planting of Orenge trees, Figge trees, Limon trees, and Almond trees; for judging how the soile may serve for the same.

9. Gardeners, to proove[42] the severall soiles of the Islands, and of our setling places, to see how the same may serve for all herbs and roots for our victualling; since by rough seas sometimes we may want fish, and since we may want flesh to victuall us, by the malice of the naturall people there: and gardeners for planting of our common trees of fruit, as Peares, Apples, Plummes, Peaches, Medlers, Apricoes, Quinces for conserves,[43] &c.

10. Lime-makers, to make lime for buildings.

11. Masons, Carpenters, &c. for buildings there.

12. Bricke-makers and Tile-makers.

13. Men cunning in the art of fortification, that may chuse out places strong by nature to be fortified, and that can plot out and direct workemen.

14. Choise Spade-men, to trench cunningly, and to raise bulwarks and rampiers of earth for defence and offence.

15. Spade-makers, that may, out of the Woods there, make spades like those of Devonshire, and of other sorts, and shovels from time to time for common use.

16. Smithes, to forge the yrons of the shovels and spades, and to make blacke billes[44] and other weapons, and to mend many things.

17. Men that use to breake Ash trees for pike-staves,[45] to be imploied in the Woods there.

18. Others, that finish up the same so rough hewd, such as in London are to be had.

19. Coopers, to make caske of all sorts.

---

[41] Farmers.

[42] To test.

[43] Medlars are soft, brown applelike fruit. Conserves are fruit preserves.

[44] A bill was a weapon consisting of a long staff with a hooked blade.

[45] The wooden shaft of a long spearlike weapon (a pike).

20. Forgers of pikes heads and of arrow heads, with forges, with Spanish yron, and with all maner of tooles to be caried with them.

21. Fletchers,[46] to renew arrowes, since archerie prevaileth much against unarmed people: and gunpowder may soone perish, by setting on fire.

22. Bowyers also, to make bowes there for need.

23. Makers of oares, since for service upon those rivers it is to great purpose, for the boats and barges they are to passe and enter with.

24. Shipwrights, to make barges and boats, and bigger vessels, if need be, to run along the coast, and to pierce the great Bayes and Inlets.

25. Turners, to turne targets[47] of Elme and tough wood, for use against the darts and arrowes of Salvages.

26. Such also as have knowledge to make targets of horne.

27. Such also as can make armor of hides upon moulds, such as were woont to be made in this realme about an hundred yeeres since, and were called Scotish jacks: such armor is light and defensive enough against the force of Salvages.

28. Tanners, to tanne hides of Buffes, Oxen, &c. in the Isles where you shall plant.

29. White Tawyers[48] of all other skinnes there.

30. Men skilfull in burning of Sope ashes, and in making of Pitch, and Tarre, and Rozen, to be fetched out of Prussia and Poland, which are thence to be had for small wages, being there in maner of slaves.

The severall sorts of trees, as Pines, Firres, Spruses, Birch and others, are to be boared with great augers a foot or halfe a yard above the ground, as they use in Vesely towards Languedock and neere Bayona in Gascoigne:[49] and so you shall easily and quickly see what Gummes, Rozen, Turpentine, Tarre, or liquor is in them, which will quickly distill out cleerely without any filthie mixture, and will shew what commoditie may be made of them: their goodnesse and greatnesse for masts is also to be considered.

31. A skilfull painter is also to be caried with you which the Spaniards used commonly in all their discoveries to bring the descriptions of all beasts, birds, fishes, trees, townes, &c.

---

[46] Arrow makers.
[47] Small round shields.
[48] Whittawers, those who taw (prepare) skins with salt and alum into whitleather, leather that is pliable and light-colored, sometimes called Hungarian leather.
[49] Gascony, a former province in southwest France.

2

RICHARD HAKLUYT (THE YOUNGER)

"Discourse of Western Planting"
1584

After the publication in 1582 of his Divers Voyages Touching the Discovery of America, *Richard Hakluyt the younger (1552?–1616) became perhaps the most active of all English promoters of overseas colonization. By the end of the 1580s he published the first edition of* The Principall Navigations, Voyages, and Traffics of the English Nation *(London, 1589), and by the end of the century he brought out his massive second edition of that work, this time in three volumes (London, 1598–1600). In all these works, Hakluyt compiled the reports of explorers to the Western Hemisphere, combined them with reports of other historic ventures (including the Crusades and numerous reports of English travelers to Russia), and printed them in the hope of encouraging the English to embrace the colonization of eastern North America.*

Perhaps as a result of the publication of Divers Voyages, *Sir Francis Walsingham, Queen Elizabeth's principal secretary and one of her advisers most interested in overseas settlements, sent Hakluyt to France in 1583 to gather materials for a report to the queen on the benefits of colonization. As secretary and chaplain to the English ambassador in Paris, Hakluyt vigorously sought out information about North America. He returned to England a year later to write "A particuler discourse concerninge the greate necessitie and manifolde comodyties that are like to growe to this Realme of Englande by the Westerne discoveries lately attempted." Though Hakluyt was only a minor official, his tract, which became known as the "Discourse of Western Planting," represented the most thorough sixteenth-century English argument for establishing colonies in America. As such, though it is a long and often cumbersome document, it reveals the great attention being paid to overseas colonization among the highest officials in England even before the defeat of the Spanish Armada in 1588. It also testifies to the enormous*

Richard Hakluyt (the younger), "A particuler discourse concerninge the greate necessitie and manifolde comodyties that are like to growe to this Realme of Englande by the Westerne discoveries lately attempted," in David Beers Quinn and Alison O. Quinn, eds., *New American World* (New York and London: Macmillan, 1979), 3:71–123.

interest America must have held for Europeans on the continent, given that Hakluyt the younger was sent to France to gather information for this report.

The document itself provides twenty-one reasons for pursuing English colonization in America. The excerpt included here begins with Hakluyt's descriptive table of contents for the entire document; it concludes with the final two chapters (20 and 21) of the original text. Like the reports of Hakluyt the elder, the "Discourse" focuses on the commodities available in the Western Hemisphere as well as the strategic advantages colonies offered. It differs from the elder Hakluyt's works in its level of detail. The younger Hakluyt was not content, as his cousin had been, to reveal the possible riches of America. In this influential position paper he informed government officials (the work was not published for another three hundred years) exactly what travelers would need to take with them to survive the ocean crossing and the types of people and goods necessary to establish successful colonies once they arrived in America. His ideas were no idle speculation; this report was, as Hakluyt intended it to be, both a justification for establishing colonies and a blueprint for creating viable settlements.

What do Hakluyt's suggestions for the necessary goods and people reveal about his plans for English colonies in North America? What products does Hakluyt expect the new colonies to yield? How will England's workforce and the unemployed benefit? How will England's economy benefit from colonization? What part does religious competition play in Hakluyt's proposal? What is Hakluyt's suggestion for maintaining discipline and a form of governance for those who voyaged to America?

---

1. That this westerne discoverie will be greately for thinlargement of the gospell of Christe whereunto the Princes of the refourmed relligion[1] are chefely bounde amongest whome her ma[tie2] ys principall.

2. That all other englishe Trades are growen beggerly or daungerous, especially in all the kinge of Spayne his Domynions, where our men are dryven to flinge their Bibles and prayer Bokes into the sea, and to forsweare and renownce their relligion and conscience and consequently theyr obedience to her Majestie.

3. That this westerne voyadge will yelde unto us all the commodities of Europe, Affrica, and Asia, as far as wee were wonte to travell, and supply the wantes of all our decayed trades.

4. That this enterprise will be for the manifolde imploymente of nom-

---

[1] Protestantism.
[2] Majesty.

bers of idle men, and for bredinge of many sufficient, and for utterance[3] of the greate quantitie of the commodities of our Realme.

5. That this voyage will be a great bridle[4] to the Indies of the kinge of Spaine and a meane that wee may arreste at our pleasure for the space of tenne weekes or three monethes every yere, one or twoo hundred saile of his subjectes shippes at the fysshinge in Newfounde lande.

6. That the mischefe that the Indian Threasure[5] wrought in time of Charles the late Emperour father to the Spanishe kinge, is to be had in consideracion of the Queenes moste excellent Majestie, leaste the contynuall commynge of the like threasure from thence to his sonne, worke the unrecoverable annoye of this Realme, whereof already wee have had very dangerous experience.

7. What speciall meanes may bringe kinge Phillippe from his high Throne, and make him equal to the Princes his neighbours, wherewithall is shewed his weakenes in the west Indies.

8. That the lymites of the kinge of Spaines domynions in the west Indies be nothinge so large as ys generally ymagined and surmised, neither those partes which he holdeth be of any such forces as ys falsly geven oute by the popishe[6] Clergye and others his fautors,[7] to terrifie the Princes of the Relligion and to abuse and blynde them.

9. The Names of the riche Townes lienge alonge the sea coaste on the northe side from the equinoctiall of the mayne lande of America under the kinge of Spayne.

10. A Brefe declaracion of the chefe Ilands in the Bay of Mexico beinge under the kinge of Spaine, with their havens and fortes, and what commodities they yelde.

11. That the Spaniardes have executed most outragious and more then Turkishe[8] cruelties in all the west Indies, whereby they are every where

---

[3] The disposal of goods by sale or barter.

[4] Restraint, i.e., the English could hinder Spanish exploration by capturing Spanish ships at will.

[5] Silver that the Spanish brought back from their explorations. English promoters often noted that the Spanish had profited handsomely from their overseas ventures, and they argued that these profits strengthened the forces of the Catholic Church.

[6] Roman Catholic.

[7] Adherents or supporters.

[8] English writers often used the example of Turkish history to illustrate any discussion of cruel and oppressive regimes. By the mid-seventeenth century, English views of the pathological tactics of Turkish leaders emerged clearly in popular histories. In the eighteenth century, colonial writers claimed that George III's acts resembled those of Turkish despots and that colonists would eventually be slaughtered en masse, their blood running in the streets, just like innocent Turks who ran afoul of their tyrannical leaders. As the historian Bernard Bailyn has noted, Turkey was "the ultimate refinement of despotism." See Bailyn, *Ideological Origins of the American Revolution* (Cambridge: Harvard University Press, 1967), 63.

there, become moste odious unto them, whoe would joyne with us or any other moste willingly to shake of their moste intollerable yoke, and have begonne to doo it already in dyvers places where they were Lordes heretofore.

12. That the passage in this voyadge is easie and shorte, that it cutteth not nere the trade of any other mightie Princes, nor nere their Contries, that it is to be perfourmed at all tymes of the yere, and nedeth but one kinde of winde, that Ireland beinge full of goodd havens on the southe and west sides, is the nerest parte of Europe to yt, which by this trade shall be in more securitie, and the sooner drawen to more Civilitie.

13. That hereby the Revenewes and customes of her Majestie bothe outwardes and inwardes shall mightely be inlarged by the toll, excises, and other dueties which withoute oppression may be raised.

14. That this action will be greately for thincrease, mayneteynaunce and safetie of our Navye, and especially of greate shippinge which is the strengthe of our Realme, and for the supportation[9] of all those occupations that depende upon the same.

15. That spedie plantinge in divers fitt places is moste necessarie upon these luckye westerne discoveries for feare of the daunger of being prevented by other nations which have the like intentions, with the order thereof and other reasons therwithall alleaged.

16. Meanes to kepe this enterprise from overthrowe and the enterprisers from shame and dishonour.

17. That by these Colonies the Northwest passage to Cathaio[10] and China may easely quickly and perfectly be searched oute aswell by river and overlande, as by sea, for proofe whereof here are quoted and alleaged divers rare Testymonies oute of the three volumes of voyadges gathered by Ramusius[11] and other grave authors.

18. That the Queene of Englande title to all the west Indies, or at the leaste to as moche as is from Florida to the Circle articke, is more lawfull and righte then the Spaniardes or any other Christian Princes.

19. An aunswer to the Bull of the Donacion[12] of all the west Indies graunted to the kinges of Spaine by Pope Alexander the vi[th] whoe was himselfe a Spaniarde borne.

20. A brefe collection of certaine reasons to induce her Majestie and the state to take in hande the westerne voyadge and the plantinge there.

---

[9] Assistance.

[10] Cathay, northern China.

[11] Giovanni Battista Ramusio (1485–1557), an Italian geographer best known for a collection of travel accounts entitled *Delle navigazioni e viaggi*, 3 vols. (1550–1559).

[12] In a papal bull (or decree) in 1493, Pope Alexander VI divided the Western Hemisphere between Spain and Portugal; Portugal received a claim to territory that became Brazil, Spain most of the rest. Protestant nations, notably England, denied the validity of the bull.

21. A note of some thinges to be prepared for the voyadge which is sett downe rather to drawe the takers of the voyadge in hande to the presente consideracion then for any other reason for that divers thinges require preparation longe before the voyadge, withoute which the voyadge is maymed.

20. A brefe Collection of certaine reasons to induce her Majestie and the state to take in hande the westerne voyadge and the plantinge there.

1. The soyle yeldeth and may be made to yelde all the severall commodities of Europe, and of all kingdomes domynions and Territories that England tradeth withe, that by trade marchandize cometh into this Realme.

2. The passage thither and home is neither to longe nor to shorte, but easie and to be made twise in the yere.

3. The passage cutteth not nere the trade of any Prince, nor nere any of their contries or Territories and is a safe passage, and not easie to be annoyed by Prince or potentate whatsoever.

4. The passage is to be perfourmed at all times of the yere, and in that respecte passeth our trades in the Levant[13] seas within the straites of Juberalter,[14] and the trades in the seas within the kinge of Denmarkes straite, and the trades to the portes of Norwey and of Russia &c., for as in the southwest straite there is no passage in sommer by lacke of windes, so within the other places there is no passage in winter by yse and extreme colde.

5. And where England nowe for certen hundredth yeres last passed by the peculiar commoditie of wolles, and of later yeres by clothinge of the same, hath raised it selfe from meaner state to greater wealthe and moche higher honour, mighte and power then before, to the equallinge of the princes of the same to the greatest potentates of this parte of the worlde, It commeth nowe so to passe that by the greate endevo[r] of the increase of the trade of wolles in Spaine and in the west Indies nowe daily more and more multiplienge, That the wolles of England and the clothe made of the same, will become base,[15] and every day more base then other, which prudently weyed, yt behoveth this Realme yf it meane not to returne to former olde meanes and basenes, but to stande in present and late former honour glorye and force, and not negligently and sleepingly to slyde into

---

[13] The eastern Mediterranean.
[14] Gibraltar.
[15] Inexpensive, cheap. Competition from Spain has forced English wool prices down.

beggery, to foresee and to plante at Norumbega[16] or some like place, were it not for any thing els but for the hope of the vent[17] of our woll indraped, the principall and in effecte the onely enrichinge contynueinge naturall commoditie of this Realme, And effectually pursueinge that course wee shall not onely finde on that tracte of lande, and especially in that firme northwarde (to whome warme clothe shalbe righte wellcome) an ample vente, but also shall from the northside of that firme finde oute knowen and unknowen Ilandes and domynions replenished with people that may fully vent the aboundance of that our commoditie that els will in fewe yeres waxe of none or of small valewe by forreine aboundaunce &c., . . .

6. This enterprise may staye the spanishe kinge from flowinge over all the face of that waste firme of America, yf wee seate and plante there in time, . . . And England possessinge the purposed place of plantinge, her Majestie may by the benefete of the seate havinge wonne goodd and royall havens, have plentie of excellent trees for mastes, of goodly timber to builde shippes and to make greate navies, of pitche, tarr, hempe, and all thinges incident for a navie royall, and that for no price and withoute money or request. Howe easie a matter may yt be to this Realme swarminge at this day with valiant youthes rustinge and hurtfull by lacke of employment, and havinge goodd makers of cable and of all sortes of cordage, and the best and moste connynge shipwrightes of the worlde to be Lordes of all those Sees, and to spoile Phillipps Indian navye, and to deprive him of yerely passage of his Treasure into Europe, and consequently to abate the pride of Spaine and of the supporter of the greate Antechriste of Rome,[18] and to pull him downe in equallitie to his neighbour princes, and consequently to cutt of the common mischefes that commes to all Europe by the peculiar aboundance of his Indian Treasure, and this withoute difficultie.

7. This voyadge albeit it may be accomplished by barke or smallest pynnesse[19] for advise or for a necessitie, yet for the distaunce, for burden and gaine in trade, the marchant will not for profitts sake use it but by shippes of greate burden, so as this Realme shall have by that meane shippes of greate burden and of great strengthe for the defence of this Realme, and for the defence of that newe seate, as nede shall require, and withall greate increase of perfecte seamen, which greate Princes in time of warres wante, and which kinde of men are neither nourished in fewe daies nor in fewe yeres.

8. This newe navie of mightie newe stronge shippes so in trade to that

---

[16] The coast of northeastern North America.
[17] Marketing, sale.
[18] The pope.
[19] Pinnace, a light sailing ship.

Norumbega and to the coastes there, shall never be subjecte to arreste of any prince or potentate, as the navie of this Realme from time to time hath bene in the portes of thempire, in the portes of the base Contries, in Spaine, Fraunce, Portingale[20] &c., in the tymes of Charles the Emperour, Fraunces the Frenche kinge and others, but shall be alwayes free from that bitter mischeefe withoute grefe or hazarde to the marchaunte, or to the state, and so alwaies readie at the commaundement of the prince, with mariners, artillory, armor, and munition ready to offende and defende as shalbe required.

9. The greate masse of wealthe of the realme imbarqued in the marchantes shippes caried oute in this newe course, shall not lightly in so farr distant a course from the coaste of Europe be driven by windes and Tempestes into portes of any forren princes, as the spanishe shippes of late yeres have bene into our portes of the weste Contries &c. and so our marchantes in respecte of private state and of the Realme in respecte of a generall safetie from venture of losse, are by this voyadge oute of one greate mischefe.

10. No forren commoditie that commes into England commes withoute payment of custome once twise or thrise before it come into the Realme, and so all forren commodities become derer[21] to the subjectes of this Realme, and by this course to Norumbega forren princes customes are avoided, and the forren commodities cheapely purchased, they become cheape to the subjectes of England to the common benefite of the people, and to the savinge of greate Treasure in the Realme, whereas nowe the Realme becommethe poore by the purchasinge of forreine commodities in so greate a masse at so excessive prices.

11. At the firste traficque[22] with the people of those partes, the subjectes of this Realme for many yeres shall chaunge many cheape commodities of these partes, for thinges of highe valour there not estemed, and this to the greate inrichinge of the Realme, if common use faile not.

12. By the greate plentie of those Regions the marchantes and their factors[23] shall lye[24] there cheape, buye and repaire their shippes cheape, and shall returne at pleasure withoute staye or restrainte of forreine Prince, whereas upon staies and restraintes the marchaunte raiseth his chardge in sale over of his ware, and buyenge his wares cheape, he may mainteine trade with smalle stocke and withoute takinge upp money upon interest, and so he shalbe riche and not subjecte to many hazardes, but

---

[20] Portugal.
[21] Dearer; i.e., more expensive.
[22] Trade or commerce.
[23] Agents.
[24] To lie, that is, live.

shalbe able to afforde the commodities for cheape prices to all subjectes of the Realme.

13. By makinge of shippes and by preparinge of thinges for the same: By makinge of Cables and Cordage, by plantinge of vines and olive trees, and by makinge of wyne and oyle, by husbandrie and by thousandes of thinges there to be don, infinite nombers of the english nation may be sett on worke to the unburdenynge of the Realme with many that nowe lyve chardgeable to the state at home.

14. If the sea coste[25] serve for makinge of salte, and the Inland for wine, oiles, oranges, lymons, figges &c., and for makinge of yron, all which with moche more is hoped, withoute sworde drawen, wee shall cutt the combe[26] of the frenche, of the spanishe, of the portingale, and of enemies, and of doubtfull frendes to the abatinge of their wealthe and force, and to the greater savinge of the wealthe of the Realme.

15. The substaunces servinge, wee may oute of those partes receave the masse of wrought wares that now wee receave out of Fraunce, Flaunders, Germanye &c. and so wee may daunte[27] the pride of some enemies of this Realme, or at the leaste in parte purchase those wares, that nowe wee buye derely of the ffrenche and Flemynge,[28] better cheape, and in the ende for the parte that this Realme was wonte to receave dryve them out of trade to idlenes for the settinge of our people on worke.

16. Wee shall by plantinge there inlarge the glory of the gospell and from England plante sincere relligion, and provide a safe and a sure place to receave people from all partes of the worlde that are forced to flee for the truthe of gods worde.

17. If frontier warres there chaunce to aryse, and if thereupon wee shall fortifie, yt will occasion the trayninge upp of our youthe in the discipline of warr, and make a nomber fitt for the service of the warres and for the defence of our people there and at home.

18. The Spaniardes governe in the Indies with all pride and tyranie; and like as when people of contrarie nature at the sea enter into Gallies, where men are tied as slaves, all yell and crye with one voice *liberta, liberta,* as desirous of libertie or freedome, so no doubte whensoever the Queene of England, a prince of such clemencie, shall seate upon that firme of America, and shalbe reported throughoute all that tracte to use the naturall people there with all humanitie, curtesie, and freedome, they will yelde themselves to her governement and revolte cleane from the Spaniarde, and specially, when they shall understande that she hath a noble

---

[25] Coast.

[26] An expression meaning to humiliate.

[27] Subdue or quell.

[28] Flemish, natives of Flanders.

navie, and that she aboundeth with a people most valiaunte for theyr defence, and her Majestie havinge Sir Fraunces Drake[29] and other subjectes already in credite wth the Symerons,[30] a people or greate multitude alreadye revolted from the spanishe governmente, she may with them and a fewe hundrethes of this nation trayned upp in the late warres of Fraunce and Flaunders, bringe greate thinges to passe, and that wth greate ease: and this broughte so aboute, her Majestie and her subjectes may bothe enjoye the treasure of the mynes of golde and silver, and the whole trade and all the gaine of the trade of marchandize that nowe passeth thither by the Spaniardes onely hande of all the commodities of Europe, which trade of marchandize onely were of it selfe suffycient (withoute the benefite of the rich myne) to inriche the subjectes, and by Customes to fill her Majesties coffers to the full: and if it be highe pollicie[31] to mayneteyne the poore people of this Realme in worke, I dare affirme that if the poore people of England were five times so many as they be, yet all mighte be sett on worke in and by workinge lynnen[32] and suche other thinges of marchandize as the trade in the Indies dothe require.

19. The present shorte trades[33] causeth the maryner[34] to be cast of, and ofte to be idle and so by povertie to fall to piracie: But this course to Norumbega beinge longer and a contynuance of themploymente of the maryner dothe kepe the maryner from ydlenes and from necessitie, and so it cutteth of the principall actions of piracie, and the rather because no riche praye for them to take commeth directly in their course or any thing nere their course.

20. Many men of excellent wittes and of divers singuler giftes overthrowen by suertishippe,[35] by sea or by some folly of youthe, that are not able to live in England may there be raised againe, and doo their Contrie goodd service: and many nedefull uses there may (to greate purpose) require the savinge of greate nombers that for trifles may otherwise be devoured by the gallowes.

21. Many souldiers and servitours in the ende of the warres that mighte be hurtfull to this Realme, may there be unladen, to the common profite and quiet of this Realme, and to our forreine benefite there as they may be employed.

---

[29] Sir Francis Drake (1540 or 1543–1596), one of the most important English explorers of the sixteenth century, made several voyages to the West Indies and completed the first English circumnavigation of the globe (1577–1580).

[30] Probably runaway slaves (from *cimarrón* in Spanish).

[31] The policy of the monarch.

[32] Linen.

[33] Inadequate trade.

[34] Mariner.

[35] Suretyship, an obligation taken by someone for another, often for payment of a debt.

22. The frye[36] of the wandringe beggars of England that growe upp ydly and hurtefull and burdenous to this Realme, may there be unladen, better bredd upp, and may people waste Contries to the home and forreine benefite, and to their owne more happy state.

23. If Englande crie oute and affirme that there is so many in all trades that one cannot live for another as in all places they doe, This Norumbega (yf it be thoughte so goodd) offreth the remedie.

21. A note of some thinges to be prepared for the voyadge, which is sett downe rather to drawe the takers of the voyadge in hande to the presente consideracion, then for any other reason for that divers thinges require preparation longe before the voyadge, withoute the which the voyadge is maymed.

DEAD VICTUALL.[37]

Hoggs fleshe barrelled & salted in greate quantitie.
Befe barrelled in lesse quantitie.
Stockfishe Meale in Barrells.
Oatemeale in barrells, nere cowched.[38]
Ryse. Sallett[39] oile. Barrelled butter.
Cheese. Hony in Barrells.
Currans. Raisons of the sonne.[40]
Dried prunes. Olives in Barrells.
Beanes, dryed on the killn.
Pease dried likewise.
Canary Wines. Hollocks.[41]
Sacks racked.[42]
Vinegar very stronge.
Aqua vitæ.[43]
Syders[44] of Fraunce, spaine, and England.
Bere brewed specially in speciall tyme.[45]

[36] Children or offspring.
[37] Food or provisions.
[38] Nearly germinated.
[39] Salad.
[40] Sun.
[41] A Spanish red wine.
[42] Stored sack, a type of white wine imported to England from the Canary Islands and Spain.
[43] Distilled spirits such as brandy or whiskey.
[44] Ciders.
[45] In its season.

VICTUALL BY ROOTES AND HERBES.

Turnep seede.
Passeneape[46] sede.
Radishe.
Cariott.
Naviewes.[47]
Garlicke.
Onyons.
Leekes.
Melons.
Pompions.[48]
Cowcombers.[49]
Cabage cole.
Parseley.
Lettis.
Endiffe.[50]
Alexander.[51]
Orege.[52]
Tyme.
Rosemary.
Mustard seede.
Fennell.
Anny seedes newe and freshe to be sowen.

THE ENCREASE RENEWE Y[e] CONTINEWE
OF VICTUALL AT THE PLANTINGE PLACES, &
MEN AND THINGES INCIDENT
AND TENDINGE TO THE SAME.

Bores, Sowes.[53]
Conies[54] bucke & dowe.
Doves male & female.
Cockes. Hennes.
Duckes male & female for lowe soiles.

---

[46] Parsnip.
[47] Rape or coleseed (a plant in the broccoli family).
[48] Pumpkins.
[49] Cucumbers.
[50] Endive, a salad green.
[51] A vegetable like celery.
[52] Oregano.
[53] Boars, or male pigs, and sows, female pigs.
[54] Rabbits.

Turkies male and female.

Wheat. Rye. Barley. ⎫ To sowe, to
Bigge or burley bere. ⎪ vittell[55] by
Oates. Beanes. ⎬ breade and
Pease. Facches.[56] ⎪ drinke,
Three square graine. ⎭ &c.

Sugar cane planters with the plantes.

Vyne planters.

Olyve planters.

Gardiners for herbes rootes, and for all earthe frutes.

Graffers[57] for frute trees.

Hunters skilfull to kill wilde beasts for vittell.

Warryners[58] to breede conies & to kill vermyn.

Fowlers.

Sea fisshers.

Freshwater fisshers.

Knytters of netts.

Butchers.

Salters and seasoners of vittell.

Saltemakers.

Cookes.

Bakers.

Brewers.

Greyhoundes to kill deere &c.

Mastives[59] to kill heavie beastes of ravyne[60] and for nighte watches.

Bloude houndes to recover hurte dere.

PROVISIONS TENDINGE TO FORCE.

Men experte in the arte of fortification.

Platformes of many formes redied to carry with you by advise of the best.

Capitaines of longe and of greate experience.

Souldiers well trayned in Flaunders to joyne with the younger.

Harqubusshiers[61] of skill.

Archers stronge bowmen.

---

[55] Victual, to provide.

[56] Presumably beans.

[57] Grafters, those who graft, or attach, branches from one plant to another.

[58] Warreners, those who raise rabbits.

[59] Mastiffs, large dogs.

[60] Ravin, prey.

[61] Soldiers armed with the harquebus, an early portable gun that could be as small as a musket or as large as a cannon.

Bowyers.[62]

Fletchers.[63]

Arrowheadmakers.

Bowstave preparers.

Glewmakers.

Morryce pikemakers and of halbert staves.[64]

Makers of spades and shovells for pyoners,[65] trentchers, and fortemakers.

Makers of basketts to cary earthe to fortes and Rampiers.

Pioners and spademen for fortificacion.

Salte peter[66] makers.

Gonne powder makers.

Targett makers of hornes[67] defensive againste Savages.

Oylethole doublett[68] makers defensive lighte and gentle to lye in.

Turners of Targetts of elme and of other toughe wooads lighte.

Shippes, Pynesses, Barkes, Busses[69] with flatt botoms furnished with experte seamen.

Swifte boates and barges to passe by winde & oare covered with quilted canvas of defence againste shott from the shoare to perce Ryvers for discoverie, and to passe to & froe offensive and defensive againste savages devised by Master Bodenham of Spaine.

Shipwrightes in some nomber to be employed on the Timber.

Oaremakers, and makers of Cable and Cordage.

PROVISIONS INCIDENT TO THE FIRSTE
TRAFICQUE AND TRADE OF MARCHANDIZE.

Grubbers and rooters upp of Cipres, Cedars, and of all other faire trees for to be employed in coffers deskes &c. for traficque.

Mattocks[70] narrowe and longe of yron to that purpose.

Millwrightes to make milles for spedy and cheape sawinge of timber and boordes for trade and firste traficque of suertie.[71]

Millwrightes for corne milles.

---

[62] Those who make bows.
[63] Those who make arrows.
[64] A morris-pike was a long-handled spear, supposedly of Moorish origin; a halbert was a weapon combining a spear with a battle-ax. Staves are staffs or shafts.
[65] Pioneers, in this context trench diggers who cleared land for foot soldiers.
[66] Potassium nitrate, a chief ingredient in gunpowder.
[67] Targets and horns were shields used in combat.
[68] Eyelets in doublets (close-fitting jackets).
[69] A two- or three-masted fishing boat.
[70] Tools used for loosening hard ground or uprooting trees.
[71] Surety; i.e., settlers who were in suretyship (see note 35).

Sawyers[72] for common use.

Carpinters for buildinges.

Joyners to cutt oute the boordes into chestes to be imbarqued for England.

Blacksmithes to many greate and nedefull uses.

Pitche[73] makers.

Tarr makers.

Burners of asshes for the trade of sope asshes.[74]

Cowpers[75] for barrells to inclose those asshes.

Tallowchandlers[76] to prepare the Tallowe to be incasked for England.

Waxechandlers to prepare waxe in like sorte.

Diers to seeke in that firme that riche Cochinilio[77] and other thinges for that trade.

Mynerall men.[78]

ARTESANES SERVINGE OUR FIRSTE PLANTERS
NOT IN TRAFICQUE BUT FOR BUILDINGES.

Brickmakers.

Tilemakers.

Lyme makers.

Bricklayers.

Tilers.

Thackers[79] wth reede, russhes, broome or strawe.

Synkers of welles and finders of springes.

Quarrellers[80] to digge Tile.

Roughe Masons.

Carpinters.

Lathmakers.[81]

ARTESANES SERVINGE OUR FIRSTE PLANTERS
AND IN PARTE SERVINGE FOR TRAFICQUE.

Barbors.

Launders.

---

[72] Those who saw timber.

[73] A dark, resinous substance used to protect wood from moisture.

[74] The ash from certain kinds of trees was used to make lye for soap.

[75] Coopers, i.e., barrel makers.

[76] Those who make or sell tallow (animal fat) or candles made from tallow.

[77] Cochineal, a dyestuff consisting of the dried bodies of *Coccus cacti,* an insect found on several species of cactus; it produces a brilliant scarlet dye.

[78] Miners.

[79] Roof thatchers.

[80] Quarriers, those who quarry stone.

[81] Those who prepare laths, wooden slats used as a base for tiles or plaster.

Tailors.
Botchers.[82]
Pailemakers.
Burrachiomakers.[83]
Bottlemakers of London.
Shoemakers. Coblers.
Tanners. White tawyers.[84]
Buffe skynne dressers.[85]
Shamew skynne dressers.[86]

A PRESENT PROVISION FOR RAISINGE
A NOTABLE TRADE FOR THE TIME TO COME.

The knitt wollen cappe of Toledo in Spaine called *bonetto rugio collerado* so infinitely solde to the Moores in Barbarie[87] and Affricke, is to be prepared in London, Hereforde, and Rosse, and to be vented to the people, and may become a notable trade of gaine to the marchaunte, and a greate reliefe to oure poore people, and a sale of our woll & of our labour, and beinge suche a cappe that every particuler person will buye and may easelie compasse, the sale wilbe great in shorte time, especially if our people weare them at their first arryvall there.

THINGES FORGOTTEN MAY HERE BE NOTED AS THEY COME
TO MYNDE AND AFTER BE PLACED WITH THE REST, AND AFTER THAT
IN ALL BE REDUCED INTO THE BEST ORDER.

That there be appointed one or twoo preachers for the voyadge that God may be honoured, the people instructed, mutinies the better avoided, and obedience the better used, that the voyadge may have the better successe.

That the voyadge be furnished with Bibles and with bookes of service.

That the bookes of the discoveries and conquestes of the easte Indies be carried with you.

That the bookes of the discoveries of the West Indies and the conquestes of the same be also caried to kepe men occupied from worse cogitations, and to raise their myndes to courage and highe enterprizes

---

[82] A mender.

[83] Makers of borachios, leather bags used in Spain for wine.

[84] Whittawers, those who taw (prepare) skins with salt and alum into whitleather, leather that is pliable and light-colored, sometimes called Hungarian leather.

[85] Those who prepare buff leather, a sturdy, whitish-yellow leather.

[86] Those who prepare the soft, pliable leather chamois.

[87] A region in North Africa extending from the west of Egypt to the Atlantic Ocean.

and to make them lesse careles for the better shonnynge[88] of common daungers in suche cases arisinge.

And because men are more apte to make themselves subjecte in obedience to prescribed lawes sett downe and signed by a prince, then to the changeable will of any Capitaine be he never so wise or temperate, never so free from desire of revenge, it is wisshed that it were learned oute what course bothe the Spaniardes and Portingales tooke in their discoveries for government, and that the same were delivered to learned men, that had perused moste of the lawes of thempire and of other princes Lawes, and that thereupon some speciall orders fitt for voyadges and begynnynges, mighte upon deliberation be sett downe and allowed by the Quenes moste excellent majestie and her wise counsell and faire ingrossed[89] mighte in a Table be sett before the eyes of suche as goe in the voyadge, that no man poonished or executed may justly complaine of manifeste and open wronge offred.

That some phisition[90] be provided to minister by counsell and by phisicke[91] to kepe and preserve from sicknes, or by skill to cure suche, as fall into disease and destemperature.[92]

A Surgeon to lett bloude and for such as may chaunce by warres or otherwise to be hurte is more nedefull for the voyage.

An Apothecarye[93] to serve the phisition is requisite, and the phisition dienge, he may chaunce (well chosen) to stande in steede of the one and thother, and to sende into the Realme by seede and roote herbes and plantes of rare excellencie.

If suche plentie of honye be in these Regions as is saied, yt were to goodd purpose to cary in the voyadge, suche of the servauntes of the Russia Companie[94] as have the skill to make the drincke called meth,[95] which they use in Russia and Poland, and nerer as in North Wales for their wine, and if you cannot cary any suche, to cary the order of the makinge of yt in writinge that it may be made for a nede.

And before many thinges this one thinge is to be called as yt were with spede to mynde, that the prisons and corners of London are full of decayed marchantes overthrowen by losse at sea, by usuerers,[96] suertishippe and

---

[88] Shunning, avoidance.

[89] Engrossed, expressed or written in a legal document.

[90] Physician.

[91] Medicine.

[92] Distemper, a sickness believed to be caused by an imbalance of the humors, or fluids, in the body.

[93] Someone who prepared and sold medicines.

[94] The English trading company chartered to trade in Russia.

[95] Metheglin, or mead, a liquor made from honey and water.

[96] A usurer was a money lender, typically someone who charged excessive interest on loans.

by sondry other suche meanes, and dare or cannott for their debtes shewe their faces, and in truthe many excellent giftes be in many of these men, and their goodd giftes are not ymployed to any manner of use, nor are not like of themselves to procure libertie to employe themselves. But are withoute some speciall meane used to starve by wante, or to shorten their tymes by thoughte, and for that these men, schooled in the house of adversitie, are drawen to a degree higher in excellencye, and may be employed to greate uses in this purposed voyadge, yt were to greate purpose to use meanes by aucthoritie for suche as maliciously, wrongfully or for triflinge causes are deteyned, and to take of them and of others that hide their heades and to employe them, for so they may be relieved and the enterprice furthered in many respectes.

And in choice of all Artesanes for the voyadge this generall rule were goodd to be observed that no man be chosen that is knowen to be a papiste[97] for the speciall inclynation they have of favour to the kinge of Spaine.

That also of those Artesanes which are protestantes, that where you may have chaunge and choice; that suche as be moste stronge and lusty men be chosen, and suche as can best handle his Bowe and his har-quebushe; for the more goodd giftes that the goers in the voyadge have, the more ys the voyadge benefited. And therefore (many goinge) yf every mans giftes and goodd qualities be entred into a Booke before they be receaved, they may be employed upon any necessitie in the voyadge in this or in that, accordinge as occasion of nede shall require.

---

[97] A Roman Catholic, a follower of the pope.

3

GEORGE PECKHAM

A True Reporte
of the Late Discoveries . . .
by . . . Sir Humphrey Gilbert

1583

In the late sixteenth century, Sir Humphrey Gilbert (1539?–1583) was among the most important English explorers of the Atlantic world. Along with Sir Francis Drake and Sir Walter Ralegh (who was also Gilbert's stepbrother), he promoted the twin goals of finding a northwest passage to China and of encouraging settlement in northeastern North America. In the mid-1570s he published a remarkable tract entitled A Discourse of a Discoverie for a New Passage to Cataia *(London, 1576), a report he had first written a decade earlier reflecting English desires for a water route to China. Although the work was brazenly promotional and exaggerated, it fueled others' interest. Gilbert was already an experienced colonizer; he had been among the first leaders of the often bloody Elizabethan campaign to subdue the Irish in the 1560s. In the late 1570s he had set out across the Atlantic for the first time. Though he returned from that venture, he never lived to find out if the passage to China existed or to establish colonies on North American soil: He vanished at sea on a subsequent return voyage to England in 1583.*

Among the promoters who advanced Gilbert's ideas before and after his death was Sir George Peckham (d. 1608), who wrote this report about Gilbert's explorations. Peckham had been involved with Gilbert since 1574 when, together with Sir Richard Grenville (Ralegh's cousin, who commanded an expedition to Roanoke) and Christopher Carleill (son-in-law of Sir Francis Walsingham, an adviser to the queen), they petitioned Queen Elizabeth for land in North America. Gilbert received a patent, an exclusive license to control a particular area, in 1578, and he granted Peckham a large tract near Narragansett Bay as well as the freedom to trade there.

Sir George Peckham, *A True Reporte of the Late Discoveries and Possession . . . of the Newfound Landes . . . by . . . Sir Humphrey Gilbert*, in David Beers Quinn and Alison O. Quinn, eds., *New American World*, 5 vols. (London: Macmillan, 1979), 3:34–60.

Peckham, a Catholic, hoped with others to establish a refuge for English Catholics who felt persecuted in a Protestant nation. But he was unable to sustain interest in this project and eventually worked with others to promote a nonsectarian colony in North America. In spite of receiving word about Gilbert's probable demise, Peckham published A True Reporte of the Late Discoveries and Possession, Taken in the Right of the Crown of Englande, of the Newfound Landes: by That Valiant and Worthye Gentleman, Sir Humphrey Gilbert *(London, 1583).*

In the work, two passages of which are printed here, Peckham put forth several of the standard arguments for colonization: He drew on Scripture (particularly the book of Joshua) to justify his ideas; he compared English claims to those of the Spanish; and he emphasized that trade would benefit both America's natives and the English nation. Like the Hakluyts, with whose work he was familiar, Peckham enumerated the commodities to be found in America as well as the types of migrants who could establish the most profitable colony. In the passages included here, Peckham laid out the benefits of English colonization and outlined his plans for creating a feudal society in North America. He argued that the colony would not be an economic burden to the realm but a profitable venture that would help ameliorate some of England's pressing domestic problems. Although this settlement would draw from the general English population, it is clear that Peckham hoped to attract even wealthy members of the nation.

What, in Peckham's view, were the chief benefits to the Indians from colonization? Do you think his arguments were genuine or self-serving? What English people did Peckham think would populate the colonies? Why did he think it would not cost as much to equip an expedition to North America as some other commentators thought it would? How realistic were Peckham's ideas? What was the feudal structure that Peckham envisioned for the new colonies? Why do you think he proposed this structure? How did this structure differ from that proposed by other writers?

The sixt Chapter, sheweth that the Traffique[1] and Planting in those Countries, shall be unto the Savages themselves verie beneficiall and gainefull.

Now to the end it may appeare, that this voiage is not undertaken altogether for the peculiar commoditie of our selves, and our Countrie, (as generallie other trades and journeies be) it shall fall out in proofe, that the

---

[1] Trade or commerce.

Savages shal heerby have just cause to blesse the howre, when this enterprise was undertaken.

First and cheefly, in respect of the most happy and gladsome tydings of the most gracious Gospel of our Saviour Jesus Christ, whereby they may be brought from falsehood to truth, from darknes to lyght, from the hieway of death, to the path of life, from superstitious idolatry, to sincere Christianity, from the devill to Christ, from hell to Heaven. And if in respect of all the commodities they can yeeld us (were they many moe) that they should but receyve this only benefite of christianity, they were more then fully recompenced.

But heerunto it may be objected, that the Gospel must be freely preached, for such was the example of the Apostles, unto whom although the aucthorities and examples before alledged, of Emperors, Kings, and Princes, as wel before Christes time as since, might sufficiently satisfie: Yet for further aunswer, we may say with Saint Paule. If we have sowen unto you heavenlie thinges, doo you thinke it much that we should reape your carnall thinges? And withall, The workman is worthy of his hier.[2] These heavenly tydings which those labourers our countreymen (as messengers of Gods great goodnes and mercy) wyl voluntarily present unto them, dooth farre exceed their earthly ritches. Moreover, if the other inferior worldlie, and temporall thinges, which they shal receive from us, be waied[3] in equal balance, I assure my selfe, that by equall judgement of any indifferent person, the benefites which they then receive, shall far surmount those which they shall depart withall unto us. And admitte that they had (as they have not) the knowledge to put theyr land to some use: Yet being brought from brutish ignoraunce, to civility and knowledge, and made them to understand how the tenth part of their land may be so manured and emploied, as it may yeeld more commodities to the necessary use of mans life, then the whole now dooth: What just cause of complaint may they have? And in my private opinion, I doo verily think that God did create lande, to the end that it shold by Culture and husbandrie, yeeld things necessary for mans lyfe.

But this is not all the benefit which they shall receive by the christians, for, over and beside the knowledge how to tyl and dresse their grounds, they shalbe reduced from unseemly customes, to honest maners, from disordred riotous rowtes[4] and companies, to a wel governed common wealth, and withall shalbe taught mecanicall occupations, artes, and lyberal Sciences: and which standeth them most upon, they shalbe defended from

---

[2] Hire.
[3] Weighed.
[4] Routs, disorderly, disreputable crowds.

the cruelty of their tyrannicall and blood sucking neighbors, the Canniballes,[5] wherby infinite number of their lives shalbe preserved. And lastly, by this meanes many of their poore innocent children shalbe preserved from the bloody knife of the sacrificer, a most horrible and detestable custome in the sight of God and man, now and ever heertofore used amongst them. Many other thinges could I heere alledge to this purpose, were it not that I doo feare least I have already more than halfe tired the Reader.

The seaventh Chapter sheweth that the Planting there, is not a matter of such charge or diffycultie, as many would make it seeme to be.

Now therefore for proofe, that the Planting in these parts is a thing that may be doone without the aide of the Princes power and purse, contrarye to the allegation of many malicious persons, who will neither be actors in any good action themselves, nor so much as afoord a good word to the setting forward thereof: and that wurse, is they wyl take upon them to make Molehylles seeme Mountaines, and flies Elephants, to the end they may discourage others, that be verye well or indifferently affected to the matter, being like unto Esoppes Dogge[6] which neither would eate haie himself, nor suffer the poore hungry asse to feede thereon.

I say and affirme that God hath provided such meanes for the furtheraunce of this enterprise, as doth stande us in steede of great treasure: for first by reason that it hath pleased God of his great goodnesse, of long time to holde his merciful hand over this Realme, in preserving the people of the same, both from slaughter by the sword, and great death by plague, pestilence, or otherwise, there is at this day great numbers (God he knoweth) which live in such penurie and want, as they could be contented to hazarde their lives, and to serve one yeere for meate, drinke, and apparel, onely without wages, in hope thereby to amend theyr estates: which is a matter in such lyke journeis, of no small charge to the Prince. Moreover, thinges in the lyke journeis of greatest price and cost, as victual[7] (whereof there is great plenty to bee had in that countrye without money) and powder, great artillery, or Corselets,[8] are not needful, in so

---

[5] By the mid-sixteenth century, the English used this word, originally the proper name of the cannibalistic Caribs of the Antilles, to refer to any Indians who they feared would kill or eat them.

[6] Aesop's dog; a reference to Aesop's tale of the dog in the manger, in which the dog prevents an ass from eating hay although the hay is of no use to the dog.

[7] Food, provisions.

[8] Suits of armor that cover the body.

plentiful and chargeable manner, as the shew of such a journey, may present, for a smal quantity of all these to furnish the Forte onely wyl suffice, untyl such time as divers commodities may be found out in those parts, which may be thought wel woorthy a greater charge. Also the peculiar benefite of Archers which God hath blessed this land withal, before al other nations, will stand us in great stede amongst those naked people.

Another helpe we have also, which in such lyke cases is a matter of mervailous[9] cost, and wil be in this journey procured very easily (that is to say) To transport yeerely as wel our people, as al other necessaries, needful for them into those parts by the Fleete of Merchaunts, that yeerely venture for Fish in Newfound Land, being not farre distaunt from the countrey, meant to be inhabited, who commonly go with empty Vesselles in effect, saving some lyttle fraught with Salt. And thus it appeareth that the Souldiers wages, and the transportation may be defrayed for farre lesse summes of money, then the detractors of this enterprise have given out. Againe, this intended voiage for conquest, hath in lyke manner many other singular priviledges, wherewith God hath as it were, with his holy hand blessed the same before all others. For after once we are departed the coast of England, we may passe straight way thether, without the daunger of being driven into any the countries of our enimies, or doubtfull freends, for commonly one winde serveth to bring us thether, which sildome faileth from the middle of Januarie, to the middle of Maie, a benefite which the Mariners make great account off, for it is a pleasure that they have in few or none of the other journies. Also, the passage is short, for we may go thither in thirty or forty daies at the most, having but an indifferent winde, and returne continually in sixteene or twenty dayes at the most. And in the same our journey, by reason it is in the Occean, and quite out of the way from the intercourse of other countries: we may safely trade and traffique, without perill of pyracie, neither shal our Ships, people, or goods, ther be subjecte to the arrest or molestation of any Pagan Potentate, Turkishe Tyrant, yea, or christian Prince, which heertofore, sometimes upon slender occasion in other parts, have staied our Shippes and marchaundizes, whereby great numbers of our Countrimen have beene utterly undoone, dyvers put to raunsome, yea and some lost their lives: a thing so fresh in memory as it needeth no proofe, and well worthy of consideration.

Besides, in this voyage, we doo not crosse the burnt line,[10] whereby commonly both beverage and victuall are corrupted, and mens health very

[9] Marvelous.
[10] The equator.

much impaired, neither doo we passe the frozen Seas, which yeelde sundrye extreme daungers: but have a temperate Climate at all times of the yeere, to serve our turnes. And lastly, there neede no delayes by the way, for taking in of freshwater and Fewell, (a thing usually doone in long journeys) because as I said above, the voyage is not long, and the fresh waters taken in there, our men heere in England, at theyr returne home, have found so holesome and sweete, that they have made choise to drinke it before our Beere or Ale. . . .

THE RATYFICATYON OF FORMER ADVENTURERS.

Every person which hath adventured with Sir Humfrey Gilbert Knight, or with any principall assigne from him, shall have and enjoy all such Lands, Liberties, Freedomes, Priveleges and commodities as to any of them hath beene graunted, or covenaunted by the said Sir Humfrey, or by any principall assigne, in writing to bee shewed under his or theyr handes and seales.

REWARDS TO SUCH AS HAVE ADVENTURED IN PERSON IN THE LAST VOYAGE. ASSOCYATS.

And every person which hath adventured himselfe in the last voyage, and continued in the same, until such time as the admirall of the sayd voyage was lost, and will adventure himselfe in this next voeage, shall in recompence have his rate doubled.

1. Everie person, that shall adventure in this next voyage, in money or commodityes, the some of one hundreth poundes and receyved by the treasurer, or agent to be kept in a Storehouse, provided for that purpose: shal beare the name of an associate, he, his heires and fower[11] of his servaunts serving him seven yeeres, to have free libertie to trade and trafique in the said Countries. And shall have a just portion accordyng to the quantity of his adventure, of all commodities gotten and retourned into England, by any the Vessels which shall be set forth by the sayde principall assigne, before the twenteth of March next, in Anno 1583.

2. He shall have to him and his heyres for ever, sixteene thousand acres of Land, there to bee peopled and manured at his pleasure, holding the same in socage tenner[12] by Fealtie[13] onely, with aucthoritie to keepe Court Leete, and Court Barron[14] uppon the same, at his pleasure, with as

---

[11] Four.

[12] Socage tenure, the holding of land by performing agricultural, not military, services.

[13] The obligation of fidelity on the part of a feudal tenant or vassal to his lord.

[14] Court leet and court baron were court sessions held by feudal lords; the associate granted land would be entitled to hold such sessions.

great roialties in as large and ample maner as any Associate there, or other Subject in this Realme now enjoyeth any landes in England.

3. Hee to bee chosen for one of the cheefest persons for making of Lawes there. And shall be free from all arrestes, tortures, and execution by Marshall Lawe.

4. Yeelding and paying yeerely, tenne shillinges for everye thousand acres after the same shall bee possessed and occupyed one whole yeere and to the Queenes majestie the fift part of Golde and Sylver Ower,[15] which shall bee cleerely gotten, one other fift part of Golde, Sylver, Ower, Pearle and Precious stones, to Sir Humfrey Gylbert and his heires, and to the principall assigne the like fift part, and also one fift part of Christall[16] to the said principal assigne to be found and clearely gotten upon the same sixteene thousand acres.[17]

5. There shalbe levied within three yeeres after the sayd Land shalbe inhabited, for every acre manured on[18] halfepeny yeerely for the building of Fortes, Townes, Churches Shippes, maintenaunce of learning and Soldiers, and releeving of maimed persons etc., to bee bestowed and imployed at the discretion of the principall Assigne and his heyres, the Lieftenaunt and Associate, there for the time beeing.

ASSYSTANTS.

1. Every person adventuring as aforesayde the some of fifty poundes, shall beare the name of an Assistant he and his heires males, and three of his servauntes serving him seven yeeres, to have free liberty to trade, as in the first Article of Associates.

2. He shal have to him and his heires for ever eight thousand acres of Lande, to bee peopled and manured as aforesayd, holding the same as aforesayd, with free liberty to keepe Court Leete, and courte Baron at his pleasure, and to take the commodities thereunto belonging.

3. Yeelding and paying as in the fourth Article of the Associates.

4. To be levied one halfpeny yeerelie for everie acre, as in the fift Article of the Associates.

ADVENTURERS IN THE FIRST DEGREE.

1. Every person adventuring as aforesaid; the some of xxv. pound shalbe an adventurer of the first degree he and his heires males, and two

---

[15] Ore.

[16] Crystal.

[17] Peckham here outlined the payments that landholders owed to Gilbert or his heirs and the queen each year: a minimal rent to Gilbert and a large share of any mineral resources discovered on their property, to be paid equally to Gilbert and the queen.

[18] One.

of his servauntes, serving him seaven yeeres, to be free of trade etc. as in the first Article of the Associates.

2. He shall have to him and his heires for ever, four thousand acres of Lande, to be peopled and manured as aforesaide, holding the same as aforesaid, with free liberty to keepe Court Barron at his pleasure, and to take the commodities thereunto belonging.

3. Yeelding and paying as aforesaid, and over and above to the principall assigne the tenth part of Copper.

4. To be levied one halfpeny yeerely as aforesaid.

ADVENTURERS IN THE SECOND DEGREE.

1. Every person adventuring, as aforesaid of some of xii. pound x. shillings, shalbe an adventurer of the second degree, hee and his heires males and one of his servauntes servinge him seven yeeres, to be free of trade, etc. as in the first article of the associates.

2. He shall have to him and his heires for ever two thousand acres of land, to bee peopled and manured as aforesaid, holding the same as aforesaid.

3. Yeelding and paying as aforesaid, in the third article of the adventurers of the first degree.

4. To be levied one halfpeny yeerelie as aforesaid.

GENERALL.

The generall and admirall in this voyage, shall have in all thinges as an associate, with double quantity of Land, the Leiftenaunt and Viceadmirall in quantity of Land as an associate, and in priviledges as an assistant.

CAPTAINS AND MAYSTERS.

Every Captaine, and Maister of a ship in the said voyage, shall have as an assistant.

Every Ma.[19] his mate, Ma. Carpenter and Ma. Gonner,[20] and quarter Ma shall have in Land as an assistant, and in priviledges as an adventurer of the first degree.

Every skilfull man in trying of minerall matters, and every apoticarie skilful in choise of drugges, shall have in Land as an assistant, and in priviledges as an adventurer of the first degree.

Every Gunners and Carpenters mates, Steward, Surgion, Boteswane,[21] Purser, Trumpeter and other Officer and necessarie arti-

---

[19] Master.
[20] Gunner.
[21] Boatswain, an officer on a ship in charge of the sails and rigging.

ficer,[22] having their necessary instrumentes and tooles, shall have according to the rate of Landes as an adventurer of the first degree, and in previledges as an adventurer of the second degree.

SOLDIOURS.

Every Soldiour and Mariner shall have in all thinges as an adventurer of the second degree.

Every Person that shall winter and remaine in those Countries, one whole yeere shall have double the quantity of Land, as by this rate hee ought to have, if hee did not stay one yeere as aforesaid.

These rewardes to be extended to those persons only, which shall travell in the sayd voyage for, their thirds or shares uppon their owne adventures without wages and not to any others.

Every person, who shalbe willing to adventure in commodities, as aforesaid under the some of xii. pound x. shillinges shall have freedome of trad, land and liberties rated, according to the proporcion of his adventure.

Every person which hath, or shall adventure in this voyage in money or commodities as aforesaid, and will also adventure his person in this next voyage, shall have in respect of his person according to the rate aforesaid, over and above his adventure.

---

[22] Artisan, craftsman.

4

THOMAS HARRIOT

A Briefe and True Report
of the New Found Land
# of Virginia
1590

The 1590 edition of Thomas Harriot's A Briefe and True Report of the New Found Land of Virginia *was perhaps the single most important sixteenth-century promotional work relating to North America. It combined the most realistic description of American peoples and resources with a series of engravings illustrating the Carolina Algonquian Indians and their customs. Though it first appeared in a quarto edition of 1588 and again in Hakluyt's* Principall Navigations *in 1589, neither of these editions had the impact of the folio edition of 1590 published by the printer Theodore de Bry, who included a series of his own engravings based on the paintings of John White. The importance of the visual material was certainly not lost on de Bry, who printed the 1590 edition in four languages (German, French, and Latin as well as English). Here was a work to enlighten Europeans about the realities of life in America. In many ways, Harriot's* True Report *was an appropriate work to receive such attention.*

Though a young man in 1585 when he went to Roanoke Island (off the coast of modern-day North Carolina), Harriot (1560–1621) eventually became a leading mathematician and one of England's foremost scientists. Foreshadowing his later skills, his Report *described in detail the flora and fauna of the region. Apparently Harriot's astronomical observations helped White draw what became the most accurate map of the areas of English exploration at the time. To this day, Harriot's writings and White's illustrations provide perhaps the best evidence for the lifestyles of the native inhabitants of the southeast, many of whom perished in subsequent decades through the spread of epidemic diseases. Harriot could write with precision*

Thomas Harriot, *A Briefe and True Report of the New Found Land of Virginia*, in David Beers Quinn and Alison O. Quinn, eds. *New American World*, 5 vols. (New York and London: Macmillan, 1979), 3:139–55.

about the southeastern Algonquians because he, unlike the Hakluyts, actually traveled to North America and thus witnessed for himself the peoples and resources he described. Further, as one of the few English colonists to learn Carolina Algonquian, Harriot was able to talk to the local Indians and record their ideas, including their religious beliefs.

Harriot and White were not accidental travelers to North America. They went there under the guidance of Sir Walter Ralegh, with the specific purpose of gathering information about the nascent English settlement on Roanoke. The area was part of a region termed "Virginia" after the unmarried Queen Elizabeth; that term, de Bry noted in this edition, applied to all of the territory between Florida and Cape Breton (an island east of modern-day Nova Scotia). Ralegh believed, with good reason, that Roanoke needed more support if the first English colony in North America was going to survive. The earliest settlers there, short of supplies, fared miserably in 1585 and 1586; those who remained at the end of twelve months returned to England instead of staying. But Ralegh wanted the settlement to survive, so he sent another group there in 1587, this time under the direction of White (who had been appointed governor of the colony). But White soon returned to England, leaving many of the 110 colonists behind. Because of the naval confrontation with the Spanish Armada off the coast of England and France in 1588, no English ships managed to get back to Roanoke until 1590, when the English discovered that the original colonists had disappeared.

Harriot's True Report *was intended to provide support for Roanoke at a crucial time in its history. Though it failed in that specific purpose, it nonetheless furthered Europeans' knowledge of America. Harriot's careful catalog of the resources of the area and his precise descriptions of the local Indians (with particular attention to their economy and spiritual beliefs) made Virginia more tempting than did the vague descriptions to be found in the writing of the Hakluyts. And de Bry's engravings of White's images gave to many Europeans a lasting impression of American Indians.*

How does Harriot describe the Indians' religious beliefs, and what is his attitude toward those beliefs? What were the Indians' attitudes toward the English religion? How do the Indians interpret the deaths of their people that seemed to follow the English party? How does Harriot's tone differ from that of the Hakluyts and Peckham? In what ways, according to Harriot, have other chroniclers misrepresented the conditions in the colony of Virginia? Why have they done so? How do the pictures amplify the themes of Harriot's text?

To the Adventurers, Favourers, and Welwillers of the enterprise for the inhabiting and planting in Virginia.

Since the first undertaking by Sir Walter Ralegh to deale in the action of discovering of that countrey which is now called and knowen by the name of Virginia, many voyages having beene thither made at sundry times to his great charge; as first in the yere 1584, and afterwards in the yeres 1585, 1586, and now of late this last yeere 1587: there have bene divers and variable reports, with some slanderous and shamefull speeches bruted[1] abroad by many that returned from thence: especially of that discovery which was made by the Colony transported by Sir Richard Grinvile[2] in the yere 1585, being of all others the most principall, and as yet of most effect, the time of their abode in the countrey being a whole yere, when as in the other voyage before they stayed but six weeks, and the others after were onely for supply and transportation, nothing more being discovered then had bene before. Which reports have not done a little wrong to many that otherwise would have also favoured and adventured in the action, to the honour and benefit of our nation, besides the particular profit and credit which would redound to themselves the dealers therein, as I hope by the sequel of events, to the shame of those that have avouched the contrary, shall be manifest, if you the adventurers, favourers and welwillers doe but either increase in number, or in opinion continue, or having beene doubtfull, renew your good liking and furtherance to deale therein according to the woorthinesse thereof already found, and as you shall understand hereafter to be requisit. Touching which woorthinesse through cause of the diversity of relations and reports, many of your opinions could not be firme, nor the minds of some that are well disposed be setled in any certaintie.

I have therefore thought it good, being one that have beene in the discoverie, and in dealing with the naturall inhabitants specially imployed: and having therefore seene and knowen more then the ordinary, to impart so much unto you of the fruits of our labours, as that you may know how injuriously the enterprise is slandered, and that in publique maner at this present, chiefly for two respects.

First, that some of you which are yet ignorant or doubtfull of the state thereof, may see that there is sufficient cause why the chiefe enterpriser[3] with the favour of her Majesty, notwithstanding such reports, hath not onely since continued the action by sending into the countrey againe, and

[1] Bruited, reputed.
[2] Sir Richard Grenville.
[3] Ralegh.

replanting this last yeere a new Colony, but is also ready, according as the times and meanes will affoord, to follow and prosecute the same.

Secondly, that you seeing and knowing the continuance of the action, by the view hereof you may generally know and learne what the countrey is, and thereupon consider how your dealing therein, if it proceed, may returne you profit and gaine, be it either by inhabiting and planting, or otherwise in furthering thereof.

And least that the substance of my relation should be doubtfull unto you, as of others by reason of their diversitie, I will first open the cause in a few words, wherefore they are so different, referring my selfe to your favourable constructions, and to be adjudged of, as by good consideration you shall finde cause.

Of our company that returned, some for their misdemeanour and ill dealing in the countrey have bene there worthily punished, who by reason of their bad natures, have maliciously not onely spoken ill of their Governours, but for their sakes slandered the countrey it selfe. The like also have those done which were of their consort.

Some being ignorant of the state thereof, notwithstanding since their returne amongst their friends & acquaintance, and also others, especially if they were in company where they might not be gainsayd,[4] would seeme to know so much as no men more, and make no men so great travellers as themselves. They stood so much, as it may seeme, upon their credit and reputation, that having bene a twelvemoneth in the countrey, it would have bene a great disgrace unto them, as they thought, if they could not have sayd much, whether it were true or false. Of which some have spoken of more then ever they saw, or otherwise knew to be there. Other some have not bene ashamed to make absolute deniall of that, which although not by them, yet by others is most certainly and there plentifully knowen, & other some make difficulties of those things they have no skill of.

The cause of their ignorance was, in that they were of that many that were never out of the Island where we were seated, or not farre, or at the least wise in few places els, during the time of our abode in the country: or of that many, that after gold & silver was not so soone found, as it was by them looked for, had litle or no care of any other thing but to pamper their bellies: or of that many which had litle understanding, lesse discretion, and more tongue then was needfull or requisite.

Some also were of a nice bringing up, only in cities or townes, or such as never (as I may say) had seene the world before. Because there were

---

[4] Denied.

not to be found any English cities, nor such faire houses, nor at their owne wish any of their old accustomed dainty food, nor any soft beds of downe or feathers, the countrey was to them miserable, and their reports thereof according.

Because my purpose was but in briefe to open the cause of the variety of such speeches, the particularities of them, and of many envious, malicious, and slanderous reports and devices els, by our owne countrey-men besides, as trifles that are not worthy of wise men to be thought upon, I meane not to trouble you withall, but will passe to the commodi-ties, the substance of that which I have to make relation of unto you.

The Treatise whereof, for your more ready view and easier un-derstanding, I will divide into three speciall parts. In the first I will make declaration of such commodities there already found or to be raised, which will not onely serve the ordinary turnes of you which are and shall be the planters and inhabitants, but such an overplus sufficiently to be yeelded, or by men of skill to be provided, as by way of traffique[5] and exchange with our owne nation of England, will inrich your selves the providers: those that shall deale with you, the enterprisers in generall, and greatly profit our owne countreymen, to supply them with most things which heretofore they have bene faine[6] to provide either of strangers or of our enemies, which commodities, for distinction sake, I call Merchantable.

In the second I will set downe all the commodities which we know the countrey by our experience doth yeeld of it selfe for victuall[7] and suste-nance of mans life, such as are usually fed upon by the inhabitants of the countrey, as also by us during the time we were there.

In the last part I will make mention generally of such other commodities besides, as I am able to remember, and as I shall think behoovefull[8] for those that shall inhabit, and plant there, to know of, which specially concerne building, as also some other necessary uses: with a briefe description of the nature and maners of the people of the countrey.

[Harriot here enumerates the commodities to be found in "Virginia."— Ed.]

Of the nature and maners of the people.

It resteth[9] I speake a word or two of the naturall inhabitants, their natures and maners, leaving large discourse thereof until time more convenient

---

[5] Trade, commerce.
[6] Pleased.
[7] Food, provisions.
[8] Necessary.
[9] Remains to be done.

hereafter: nowe onely so farre foorth, as that you may know, how that
they in respect of troubling our inhabiting and planting, are not to be
feared, but that they shall have cause both to feare and love us, that shall
inhabite with them.

They are a people clothed with loose mantles made of deere skinnes,
and aprons of the same round about their middles, all els naked, of such a
difference of statures onely as wee in England, having no edge tooles or
weapons of yron or steele to offend us withall, neither knowe they how to
make any: those weapons that they have, are onely bowes made of
Witch-hazle, and arrowes of reedes, flat edged truncheons also of wood
about a yard long, neither have they any thing to defend themselves but
targets[10] made of barkes, and some armours made of sticks wickered
together with thread.

Their townes are but small, and neere the Sea coast but fewe, some
contayning but tenne or twelve houses; some 20. the greatest that we
have seene hath bene but of 30. houses: if they bee walled, it is onely done
with barkes of trees made fast to stakes, or els with poles onely fixed
upright, and close one by another.

Their houses are made of small poles, made fast at the tops in round
forme after the maner as is used in many arbories in our gardens of
England, in most townes covered with barkes, and in some with artificiall
mats made of long rushes, from the tops of the houses downe to the
ground. The length of them is commonly double to the breadth, in some
places they are but 12. and 16. yards long, and in other some we have
seene of foure and twentie.

In some places of the Countrey, one onely towne belongeth to the
government of a Wiroans[11] or chiefe Lord, in other some two or three, in
some sixe, eight, and more: the greatest Wiroans that yet wee had dealing
with, had but eighteene townes in his government, and able to make not
above seven or eight hundreth fighting men at the most. The language of
every government is different from any other, and the further they are
distant, the greater is the difference.

Their maner of warres amongst themselves is either by sudden surprising one an other most commonly about the dawning of the day, or
moone-light, or els by ambushes, or some subtile devises. Set battels are
very rare, except it fall out where there are many trees, where either part
may have some hope of defence, after the delivery of every arrow, in
leaping behind some or other.

If there fall out any warres betweene us and them, what their fight is

[10] Light, round shields.
[11] A chief of Virginia Indians.

likely to bee, wee having advantages against them so many maner of wayes, as by our discipline, our strange weapons and devises else, especially Ordinance[12] great and small, it may easily bee imagined: by the experience wee have had in some places, the turning up of their heeles against us in running away was their best defence.

In respect of us they are a people poore, and for want of skill and judgement in the knowledge and use of our things, doe esteeme our trifles before things of greater value: Notwithstanding, in their proper maner (considering the want of such meanes as we have), they seeme very ingenious. For although they have no such tooles, nor any such crafts, Sciences and Artes as wee, yet in those things they doe, they shew excellence of wit. And by how much they upon due consideration shall finde our maner of knowledges and crafts to exceede theirs in perfection, and speede for doing or execution, by so much the more is it probable that they should desire our friendship and love, and have the greater respect for pleasing and obeying us. Whereby may bee hoped, if meanes of good government be used, that they may in short time bee brought to civilitie, and the imbracing of true Religion.

Some religion they have already, which although it be farre from the trueth, yet being as it is, there is hope it may be the easier and sooner reformed.

They beleeve that there are many gods, which they call Mantoac, but of different sorts & degrees, one onely chiefe and great God, which hath bene from all eternitie. Who, as they affirme, when hee purposed to make the world, made first other gods of a principall order, to be as meanes and instruments to be used in the creation and government to follow, and after the Sunne, moone, and starres as pettie gods, and the instruments of the other order more principal. First (they say) were made waters, out of which by the gods was made all diversitie of creatures that are visible or invisible.

For mankinde they say a woman was made first, which by the working of one of the gods, conceived and brought foorth children: And in such sort they say they had their beginning. But how many yeeres or ages have passed since, they say they can make no relation, having no letters nor other such meanes as we to keepe Records of the particularities of times past, but onely tradition from father to sonne.

They thinke that all the gods are of humane shape, and therefore they represent them by images in the formes of men, which they call Kewaso-wok, one alone is called Kewas: them they place in houses appropriate or

---

[12] Display of military force.

temples, which they call Machicomuck, where they worship, pray, sing, and make many times offring unto them. In some Machicomuck we have seene but one Kewas, in some two, and in other some three. The common sort thinke them to be also gods.

They beleeve also the immortalitie of the soule, that after this life as soone as the soule is departed from the body, according to the workes it hath done, it is either caried to heaven the habitacle[13] of gods, there to enjoy perpetuall blisse and happinesse, or els to a great pitte or hole, which they thinke to be in the furthest parts of their part of the world toward the Sunne set, there to burne continually: the place they call Popogusso.

For the confirmation of this opinion, they tolde me two stories of two men that had bene lately dead and revived againe, the one happened but few yeeres before our comming into the Countrey of a wicked man, which having bene dead and buried, the next day the earth of the grave being seene to move, was taken up againe, who made declaration where his soule had bene, that is to say, very neere entring into Popogusso, had not one of the gods saved him, and gave him leave to returne againe, and teach his friends what they should do to avoyd that terrible place of torment. The other happened in the same yeere we were there, but in a towne that was 60. miles from us, and it was told me for strange newes, that one being dead, buried, and taken up againe as the first, shewed that although his body had lien dead in the grave, yet his soule was alive, & had travailed farre in a long broad way, on both sides whereof grew most delicate and pleasant trees, bearing more rare and excellent fruits, then ever hee had seene before, or was able to expresse, and at length came to most brave and faire houses, neere which he met his father that had bene dead before, who gave him great charge to goe backe againe, and shew his friendes what good they were to doe to enjoy the pleasures of that place, which when he had done he should after come againe.

What subtiltie soever be in the Wiroances and priestes, this opinion worketh so much in many of the common and simple sort of people, that it maketh them have great respect to their Governours, and also great care what they doe, to avoyd torment after death, and to enjoy blisse, although notwithstanding there is punishment ordeined for malefactours,[14] as stealers, whoremongers, and other sorts of wicked doers, some punished with death, some with forfeitures,[15] some with beating, according to the greatnesse of the facts.

---

[13] Dwelling place.
[14] Evildoers.
[15] Deprivation of an estate after committing a crime.

And this is the summe of their Religion, which I learned by having speciall familiaritie with some of their priests. Wherein they were not so sure grounded, nor gave such credite to their traditions and stories, but through conversing with us they were brought into great doubts of their owne, and no small admiration of ours, with earnest desire in many, to learne more then wee had meanes for want of perfect utterance in their language to expresse.

Most things they sawe with us, as Mathematicall instruments, sea Compasses, the vertue of the load-stone[16] in drawing yron, a perspective glasse[17] whereby was shewed many strange sights, burning glasses, wilde firewoorkes, gunnes, hookes, writing and reading, springclockes that seeme to goe of themselves and many other things that wee had were so strange unto them, and so farre exceeded their capacities to comprehend the reason and meanes how they should be made and done, that they thought they were rather the workes of gods then of men, or at the leastwise they had bene given and taught us of the gods. Which made many of them to have such opinion of us, as that if they knew not the trueth of God and Religion already, it was rather to bee had from us whom God so specially loved, then from a people that were so simple, as they found themselves to be in comparison of us. Whereupon greater credite was given unto that wee spake of, concerning such matters.

Many times and in every towne where I came, according as I was able, I made declaration of the contents of the Bible, that therein was set foorth the true and onely God, and his mightie workes, that therein was conteined the true doctrine of salvation through Christ, with many particularities of Miracles and chiefe points of Religion, as I was able then to utter, and thought fit for the time. And although I told them the booke materially and of it selfe was not of any such vertue, as I thought they did conceive, but onely the doctrine therein conteined: yet would many be glad to touch it, to embrace it, to kisse it, to holde it to their breastes and heads, and stroke over all their body with it, to shew their hungry desire of that knowledge which was spoken of.

The Wiroans with whom we dwelt called Wingina, and many of his people would bee glad many times to be with us at our Prayers, and many times call upon us both in his owne towne, as also in others whither hee sometimes accompanied us, to pray and sing Psalmes, hoping thereby to be partaker of the same effects which we by that meanes also expected.

Twise this Wiroans was so grievously sicke that he was like to die, and as he lay languishing, doubting of any helpe by his owne priestes, and

---

[16] Lodestone, magnetic oxide of iron; that is, a magnet attracting iron.
[17] Telescope.

thinking hee was in such danger for offending us and thereby our God, sent for some of us to pray and bee a meanes to our God that it would please him either that he might live, or after death dwell with him in blisse, so likewise were the requests of many others in the like case.

On a time also when their corne began to wither by reason of a drought which happened extraordinarily, fearing that it had come to passe by reason that in some thing they had displeased us, many would come to us and desire us to pray to our God of England, that he would preserve their Corne, promising that when it was ripe we also should be partakers of the fruit.

There could at no time happen any strange sicknesse, losses, hurts, or any other crosse unto them, but that they would impute to us the cause or meanes thereof, for offending or not pleasing us. One other rare and strange accident, leaving others, wil I mention before I end, which moved the whole Countrey that either knew or heard of us, to have us in wonderfull admiration.

There was no towne where wee had any subtile devise practised against us, wee leaving it unpunished or not revenged (because we sought by all meanes possible to win them by gentlenesse) but that within a few dayes after our departure from every such Towne, the people began to die very fast, and many in short space, in some Townes about twentie, in some fourtie, and in one sixe score, which in trueth was very many in respect of their numbers. This happened in no place that we could learne, but where we had bin, where they used some practise against us, & after such time. The disease also was so strange, that they neither knewe what it was, nor how to cure it, the like by report of the oldest men in the Countrey never happened before, time out of minde. A thing specially observed by us, as also by the naturall inhabitants themselves. Insomuch that when some of the inhabitants which were our friends, and especially the Wiroans Wingina, had observed such effects in foure or five Townes to followe their wicked practises, they were perswaded that it was the worke of our God through our meanes, and that we by him might kill and slay whom we would without weapons, and not come neere them. And thereupon when it had happened that they had understanding that any of their enemies had abused us in our journeys, hearing that we had wrought no revenge with our weapons, and fearing upon some cause the matter should so rest: did come and intreate us that we would be a meanes to our God that they as others that had dealt ill with us might in like sort die, alleadging how much it would bee for our credite and profite, as also theirs, and hoping furthermore that we would doe so much at their requests in respect of the friendship we professed them.

Whose entreaties although wee shewed that they were ungodly, affirming that our God would not subject himselfe to any such prayers and requests of men: that indeede all things have bene and were to be done according to his good pleasure as he had ordeined: and that we to shewe our selves his true servants ought rather to make petition for the contrary, that they with them might live together with us, be made partakers of his trueth, and serve him in righteousnesse, but notwithstanding in such sort, that wee referre that, as all other things, to bee done according to his divine will and pleasure, and as by his wisedome he had ordeined to be best.

Yet because the effect fell out so suddenly and shortly after according to their desires, they thought neverthelesse it came to passe by our meanes, & that we in using such speeches unto them, did but dissemble the matter, and therefore came unto us to give us thankes in their maner, that although we satisfied them not in promise, yet in deedes and effect we had fulfilled their desires.

This marveilous accident in all the Countrey wrought so strange opinions of us, that some people could not tell whether to thinke us gods or men, and the rather because that all the space of their sicknes, there was no man of ours knowen to die, or that was specially sicke: they noted also that we had no women amongst us, neither that we did care for any of theirs.

Some therefore were of opinion that we were not borne of women, and therefore not mortal, but that we were men of an old generation many yeeres past, then risen againe to immortalitie.

Some would likewise seeme to prophecie that there were more of our generation yet to come to kill theirs and take their places, as some thought the purpose was, by that which was already done. Those that were immediately to come after us they imagined to be in the aire, yet invisible and without bodies, and that they by our intreatie and for the love of us, did make the people to die in that sort as they did, by shooting invisible bullets into them.

To confirme this opinion, their Phisitions[18] (to excuse their ignorance in curing the disease) would not be ashamed to say, but earnestly make the simple people beleeve, that the strings of blood that they sucked out of the sicke bodies, were the strings wherewithall the invisible bullets were tied and cast. Some also thought that wee shot them our selves out of our pieces, from the place where wee dwelt, and killed the people in any Towne that had offended us, as wee listed,[19] howe farre distant from us

[18] Physicians.
[19] Pleased, chose.

soever it were. And other some said, that it was the speciall worke of God for our sakes, as we our selves have cause in some sort to thinke no lesse, whatsoever some doe, or may imagine to the contrary, specially some Astrologers, knowing of the Eclipse of the Sunne which we saw the same yeere before in our voyage thitherward, which unto them appeared very terrible. And also of a Comet which began to appeare but a fewe dayes before the beginning of the saide sicknesse. But to exclude them from being the speciall causes of so speciall an accident, there are further reasons then I thinke fit at this present to be alleadged. These their opinions I have set downe the more at large, that it may appeare unto you that there is good hope they may be brought through discreete dealing and government to the imbracing of the trueth, and consequently to honour, obey, feare and love us.

And although some of our company towards the end of the yeere, shewed themselves too fierce in slaying some of the people in some Townes, upon causes that on our part might easily ynough have bene borne withall: yet notwithstanding, because it was on their part justly deserved, the alteration of their opinions generally and for the most part concerning us is the lesse to be doubted. And whatsoever els they may be, by carefulnesse of our selves neede nothing at all to be feared.

The Conclusion.

Now I have (as I hope) made relation not of so few and small things, but that the Countrey (of men that are indifferent and well disposed) may bee sufficiently liked: If there were no more knowen then I have mentioned, which doubtlesse and in great reason is nothing to that which remaineth to be discovered, neither the soyle, nor commodities. As we have reason so to gather by the difference we found in our travailes,[20] for although al which I have before spoken of, have bene discovered and experimented not farre from the Sea coast, where was our abode and most of our travailing: yet sometimes as we made our journeys further into the maine[21] and Countrey; we found the soile to be fatter, the trees greater and to grow thinner, the ground more firme and deeper mould, more and larger champions,[22] finer grasse, and as good as ever we saw any in England; in some places rockie and farre more high and hilly ground, more plentie of their fruites, more abundance of beastes, the more inhabited

---

[20] Travels.
[21] Mainland.
[22] Expanses of open, level country.

with people, and of greater pollicie[23] and larger dominions, with greater townes and houses.

Why may wee not then looke for in good hope from the inner parts of more and greater plentie, as well of other things, as of those which wee have already discovered? Unto the Spaniards happened the like in discovering the maine of the West Indies. The maine also of this Countrey of Virginia, extending some wayes so many hundreds of leagues, as otherwise then by the relation of the inhabitants wee have most certaine knowledge of, where yet no Christian prince hath any possession or dealing, cannot but yeelde many kinds of excellent commodities, which we in our discovery have not yet seene.

What hope there is els to bee gathered of the nature of the Climate, being answerable to the Iland of Japan, the land of China, Persia, Jury, the Ilands of Cyprus and Candy,[24] the South parts of Greece, Italy and Spaine, and of many other notable and famous Countreys, because I meane not to be tedious, I leave to your owne consideration.

Whereby also the excellent temperature of the aire there at all seasons, much warmer then in England, and never so vehemently hot, as sometimes is under and betweene the Tropikes, or neere them, cannot be knowen unto you without further relation.

For the holsomnesse thereof I neede to say but thus much: that for all the want of provision, as first of English victuall, excepting for twentie dayes, we lived onely by drinking water, and by the victuall of the Countrey, of which some sorts were very strange unto us, and might have been thought to have altered our temperatures in such sort, as to have brought us into some grievous and dangerous diseases: Secondly the want of English meanes, for the taking of beastes, fish and foule, which by the helpe onely of the inhabitants and their meanes could not bee so suddenly and easily provided for us, nor in so great number and quantities, nor of that choise as otherwise might have bene to our better satisfaction and contentment. Some want also we had of clothes. Furthermore in al our travailes, which were most specially and often in the time of Winter, our lodging was in the open aire upon the ground. And yet I say for all this, there were but foure of our whole company (being one hundreth and eight) that died all the yeere, and that but at the latter ende thereof, and upon none of the aforesaide causes. For all foure, especially three, were feeble, weake, and sickly persons before ever they came thither, and those that knew them, much marveled that they lived so long being in that case, or had adventured to travaile.

[23] Refinement or culture.
[24] Candia, a port city of Crete.

Seeing therefore the aire there is so temperate and holsome, the soyle so fertile, and yeelding such commodities, as I have before mentioned, the voyage also thither to and fro being sufficiently experimented to be perfourmed twise a yeere with ease, and at any season thereof: And the dealing of Sir Walter Ralegh so liberall in large giving and granting lande there, as is already knowen, with many helpes and furtherances else: (The least that he hath granted hath bene five hundreth acres to a man onely for the adventure of his person) I hope there remaines no cause whereby the action should be misliked.[25]

If that those which shall thither travaile to inhabite and plant bee but reasonably provided for the first yeere, as those are which were transported the last, and being there, doe use but that diligence and care, that is requisit, and as they may with ease: There is no doubt, but for the time following, they may have victuals that are excellent good and plentie ynough, some more English sorts of cattel also hereafter, as some have bene before, and are there yet remayning, may, and shall be (God willing) thither transported. So likewise, our kinde of fruites, rootes, and hearbes, may be there planted and sowed, as some have bene already, and prove well: And in short time also they may raise so much of those sorts of commodities which I have spoken of, as shall both enrich themselves, as also others that shall deale with them.

And this is all the fruit of our labours, that I have thought necessary to advertise[26] you of at this present: What else concerneth the nature and maners of the inhabitants of Virginia, the number with the particularities of the voyages thither made, and of the actions of such as have bene by Sir Walter Ralegh therein, and there imployed, many worthy to be remembred, as of the first discoverers of the Countrey, of our Generall for the time Sir Richard Grinvil, and after his departure of our Governour there Master Ralph Lane, with divers other directed and imployed under their government: Of the Captaines and Masters of the voyages made since for transportation, of the Governour and assistants of those already transported, as of many persons, accidents, and things els, I have ready in a discourse by it selfe in maner of a Chronicle, according to the course of times: which when time shall be thought convenient, shall be also published.

Thus referring my relation to your favourable constructions, expecting good successe of the action, from him which is to be acknowledged the authour and governour, not onely of this, but of all things els, I take my leave of you, this moneth of February 1587.

[25] Unpopular.
[26] Notify.

THE TRVE PICTVRES
AND FASHIONS OF
THE PEOPLE IN THAT PAR-
TE OF AMERICA NOVV CAL-
LED VIRGINIA, DISCOWRED BY ENGLISMEN

fent thither in the years of our Lorde 1585. att the fpeciall charge and direction of
the Honourable SIR WALTER RALEGH Knigt Lord Warden
of the ftannaries in the duchies of Corenwal and Oxford who
therin hath bynne fauored and auctorifed by her
MAAIESTIE and her let-
ters patents.

Tranflated out of Latin into English by
RICHARD HACKLVIT.

DILIGENTLYE COLLECTED AND DRAOW-
ne by IHON WHITE who was fent thiter fpeciallye and for the fame pur-
pofe by the faid SIR WALTER RALEGH the year abouefaid
1585. and alfo the year 1588. now cutt in copper and firft
publifhed by THEODORE de BRY att
his wone chardges.

The arriual of the Englifhemen II.
in Virginia.

he sea coasts of Virginia arre full of Ilands, wehr by the entrance into the mayneland is hard to finde. For although they bee separated with divers and sundrie large Division, which seeme to yeeld convenient entrance, yet to our great perill we proved that they wear shallowe, and full of dangerous flatts, and could never perce opp into the mayneland, untill wee made trialls in many places with or small pinness.[1] At lengthe wee fownd an entrance uppon our mens diligent serche therof. Affter that wee had passed opp, and sayled therin for a short space we discovered a mightye river fallinge downe in to the sownde over against those Ilands, which nevertheless wee could not saile opp any thinge far by Reason of the shallewnes, the mouth therof being annoyed[2] with sands driven in with the tyde therfore saylinge further, wee came unto a Good bigg yland,[3] the Inhabitante therof as soone as they saw us began to make a great an horrible crye, as people which never[4] befoer had seene men apparelled like us, and camme away makinge out crys like wild beasts or men out of their wyts. But beenge gentlye called backe, wee offred them of our wares, as glasses, knives, babies,[5] and other trifles, which wee thougt they deligted in. Soe they stood still, and percevinge our Good will and courtesie came fawninge uppon us, and bade us welcome. Then they brougt us to their village in the iland called, Roanoac, and unto their Weroans or Prince, which entertained us with Reasonable curtesie, althoug they wear amased at the first sight of us. Suche was our arrivall into the parte of the world, which we call Virginia, the stature of bodee[6] of wich people, theyr attire, and maneer of lyuinge,[7] their feasts, and banketts,[8]
I will particullerlye declare unto yow.

[1] Pinnace, a small sailing ship. [2] Hindered. [3] Island. [4] Never. [5] Dolls or puppets.
[6] Body. [7] Burial. [8] Banquets.

A weroan or great Lorde of Virginia. III.

he Princes of Virginia are attyred in suche manner as is expressed in this figure. They weare the haire of their heades long and bynde opp the ende of the same in a knot under their eares. Yet they cutt the topp of their heades from the forehead to the nape of the necke in manner of a cokscombe, stirkinge[1] a faier longe pecher[2] of some berd att the Begininge of the creste uppun their foreheads, and another short one on bothe seides about their eares. They hange at their eares ether thicke pearles, or somwhat els, as the clawe of some great birde, as cometh in to their fansye. Moreover They ether pownes,[3] or paynt their forehead, cheeks, chynne, bodye, armes, and leggs, yet in another sorte then the inhabitantz of Florida. They weare a chaine about their necks of pearles or beades of copper, wich they muche esteeme, and therof wear they also braselets ohn their armes. Under their brests about their bellyes appeir certayne spotts, whear they use to lett themselves bloode,[4] when they are sicke. They hange before them the skinne of some beaste verye feinelye dresset in suche sorte, that the tayle hangeth downe behynde. They carye a quiver made of small rushes holding their bowe readie bent in on hand, and an arrowe in the other, readie to defend themselves. In this manner they goe to warr, or to their solemne feasts and banquetts. They take muche pleasure in huntinge of deer wherof theris great store in the contrye, for yt is fruitfull, pleasant, and full of Goodly woods. Yt hathe also store of rivers full of divers sorts of fishe. When they go to battel they paynt their bodyes in the most terible manner that thei can devise.

[1] Sticking. [2] Feather. [3] Pounce, prick, i.e., tattoo. [4] To cure sicknesses it was common practice to open a vein and "let the blood."

87

On of the chieff Ladyes of Secota. IIII.

he woemen of Secotam are of Reasonable good proportion. In their goinge they carrye their hands danglinge downe, and air dadil in a deer skinne verye excellentlye wel dressed, hanginge downe from their navell unto the mydds of their thighes, which also covereth their hynder partz. The reste of their bodies are all bare. The forr parte of their haire is cutt shorte, the rest is not over Longe, thinne, and softe, and falling downe about their shoulders: They weare a Wrrath[1] about their heads. Their foreheads, cheeks, chynne, armes and leggs are pownced.[2] About their necks they wear a chaine, ether pricked or paynted. They have small eyes, plaine and flatt noses, narrow foreheads, and broade mowths. For the most parte they hange at their eares chaynes of longe Pearles, and of some smootht bones. Yet their nayles are not longe, as the woemen of Florida. They are also deligtted with walkinge in to the fields, and besides the rivers, to see the huntinge of deers and catchinge of fische.

[1] Wreath. [2] Pounced, pricked, i.e., tattooed.

88

Their manner of careynge ther Chil- X.
dern and a tyere of the cheiffe Ladyes of the towne of Dasamonquepeuc.

n the towne of Dasemonquepeuc distant from Roanoac 4. or 5. milles, the woemen are attired, and pownced,[3] in such sorte as the woemen of Roanoac are, yet they weare noe worathes[4] uppon their heads, nether have they their thighes painted with small pricks. They have a strange manner of bearing their children, and quite contrarie to ours. For our woemen carrie their children in their armes before their brests, but they taking their sonne[5] by the right hand, bear him on their backs, holdinge the left thighe in their lefte arme after a strange, and convesnall[6] fashion, as in the picture is to bee seene.

[3] Pounced, pricked, i.e., tattooed. [4] Wreaths. [5] Son. [6] Unusual.

The Coniuerer. XI.

hey have comonlye conjurers[1] or juglers which use strange gestures, and often contrarie to nature in their enchantments: For
they be verye familiar with devils, of whome they enquier what
their enemys doe, or other suche thinges. They shave all their
heads savinge their creste which they weare as other doe, and
fasten a small black birde above one of their ears as a badge of their
office. They weare nothinge but a skinne which hangeth downe
from their gyrdle, and covereth their privityes. They weare a bagg by their side as is
expressed in the figure. The Inhabitants give great credit unto their speeche,
which oftentymes they finde to bee true.

[1] Those who conjure spirits; magicians, wizards.

The manner of makinge their boates. XII.

he manner of makinge their boates in Virginia is verye wonderfull. For wheras they want[1] Instruments of yron,[2] or other like unto ours, yet they knowe howe to make them as handsomelye, to saile with whear they liste[3] in their Rivers, and to fishe with all, as ours. First they choose some longe, and thicke tree, according to the bignes of the boate which they would frame, and make a fyre on the grownd abowt the Roote therof, kindlinge the same by little, and little with drie mosse of trees, and chipps of woode that the flame should not mounte opp to highe, and burne to muche of the lengte of the tree. When yt is almost burnt thorough, and readye to fall they make a new fyre, which they suffer to burne untill the tree fall of it owne accord. Then burninge of the topp, and bowghs of the tree in suche wyse that the bodie of the same may Retayne his just lengthe, they raise yt uppon potes[4] laid over cross wise uppon forked posts, at suche a reasonable heighte as they may handsomlye worke uppon yt. Then take they of[5] the barke with certayne shells: thy reserve the innermost parte of the lennke,[6] for the nethermost parte of the boate. On the other side they make a fyre accordinge to the lengthe of the bodye of the tree, savinge at both the endes. That which they thinke is sufficientlye burned they quenche and scrape away with shells, and making a new fyre they burne yt agayne, and soe they continne somtymes burninge and sometymes scrapinge, untill the boate have sufficient bothowmes.[7] This[8] god indueth[9] thise savage people with sufficient reason to make thinges necessarie to serve their turnes.

[1] Lack. [2] Iron. [3] Please, choose. [4] Sticks or rods. [5] Off. [6] Log. [7] Bottoms. [8] Thus.
[9] Endued, bestowed.

91

XIII.

Their manner of fishynge in Virginia.

T hey have likewise a notable way to catche fishe in their Rivers for whearas they lacke both yron,[1] and steele, they faste[2] unto their Reedes or longe Rodds, the hollowe tayle of a certaine fishe like to a sea crabb in steede[3] of a poynte, wehr with by nighte or day they stricke fishes, and take them opp into their boates. They also know how to use the prickles, and pricks of other fishes. They also make weares,[4] with settinge opp reedes or twigges in the water, which they soe plant one within another, that they growe still narrower, and narrower, as appeareth by this figure. Ther was never seene amonge us soe cunninge a way to take fish withall, wherof sondrie sortes as they fownde in their Rivers unlike unto ours. which are also of a verye good taste. Dowbtless yt is a pleasant sighte to see the people, somtymes wadinge, and goinge somtymes sailinge in those Rivers, which are shallowe and not deepe, free from all care of heapinge opp Riches for their posterite, content with their state, and livinge frendlye together of[5] those thinges which god of his bountye hath given unto them, yet without givinge hym any thankes according to his de- sarte.[6] So savage is this people, and deprived of the true knowledge of god. For they have none other then is mentionned before in this worke.

[1] Iron. [2] Fasten. [3] Instead. [4] Weirs, enclosures set in the water for catching fish. [5] Off. [6] Desert, i.e., due reward.

heir manner of feeding is in this wise. They lay a matt made of bents[1] one the grownde and sett their meate on the mids therof, and then sit downe Rownde, the men uppon one side, and the woemen on the other. Their meate is Mayze[2] sodden . . . of verye good taste, deers flesche, or of some other beaste, and fishe. They are verye sober in their eatinge, and trinkinge,[3] and consequentlye verye longe lived because they doe not oppress nature.

[1] Reeds or rushes.   [2] Maize, corn.   [3] Drinking.

Their fitting at meate.   XVI.

hen they have escaped any great danger by sea or lande, or be returned from the warr in token of Joye they make a great fyer abowt which the men, and woemen sist[5] together, holdinge a certaine fruite in their hands like unto a rownde pompion[6] or a gourde, which after they have taken out the fruits, and the seedes, then fill with smal stons or certayne bigg kernellt to make the more noise, and fasten that uppon a sticke, and singinge after their manner, they make merrie: as myselfe observed and noted downe at my beinge amonge them. For it is a strange custome, and worth the observation.

[4] Sit.   [5] Pumpkin.

94

XVII.

Their manner of prainge vvith Rat-
tels abowt te fyer.

XVIII.

Theirdanſes vvhich they vſe att their hyghe feaſtes.

t a Certayne tyme of the yere they make a great, and solemne feaste wherunto their neighbours of the townes adjoninge repayre from all parts, every man attyred in the most strange fashion they can devise havinge certayne marks on the backs to declare of what place they bee. The place where they meet is a broade playne, abowt the which are planted in the grownde certayne posts carved with heads like to the faces of Nonnes covered with theyr vayles. Then beeing sett in order they dance, singe, and use the strangest gestures they can possiblye devise. Three of the fayrest Virgins, of the companie are in the mydds, which imbrassinge[1] one another doe as yt wear turne abowt in their dancinge. All this is donne after the sunne is sett for avoydinge of heate. When they are weerye of dancinge, they goe oute of the circle, and come in untill their dances be ended, and they goe to make merrye.

[1] Embracing.

X X.

The Tovvne of Secota.

heir townes that are not inclosed with poles aire commonlye fayrer. Then suche as are inclosed, as appereth in this figure which livelye expresseth the towne of Secotam. For the howses are Scattered heer and ther, and they have gardein expressed by the letter E. wherin groweth Tobacco which the inhabitants call Uppowoc. They have also groaves wherin thei take deer, and fields wherin they sowe their corne. In their corne fields they builde as yt weare a scaffolde wher on they sett a cottage like to a rownde chaire, signiffied by F. wherin they place one to watche for there are suche nomber of fowles, and beasts, that unless they keepe the better watche, they would soone devoure all their corne. For which cause the watcheman maketh continual cryes and noyse. They sowe their corne with a certaine distance noted by H. other wise one stalke would choke the growthe of another and the corne would not come unto his rypeurs[1] G. For the leaves therof are large, like unto the leaves of great reedes. They have also a severall broade plotte C. whear they meete with their neighbours, to celebrate their cheefe solemne feastes . . . and a place D. whear after they have ended their feaste they make merrie togither. Over against this place they have a rownd plott B. wher they assemble themselves to make their solemne prayers. Not far from which place ther is a lardge buildinge A. wherin are the tombes of their kings and princes . . . likewise they have garden notted bey the letter I. wherin they use to sowe pompions.[2] Also a place marked with K. wherin the make a fyre att their solemne feasts, and hard without the towne a river L. from whence they fetche their water. This people therfore voyde of all covetousnes lyve cherfullye and att their harts ease. Butt they solemnise their feasts in the nigt, and therfore they keepe verye great fyres to avoyde darkenes, ant to testifie their Joye.

[1] Ripeness. [2] Pumpkins.

he people of this cuntrie have an Idol, which they call Kiwasa: yt is carved of woode in lengthe 4. foote whose heade is like the heades of the people of Florida, the face is of a flesh colour, the brest white, the rest is all blacke, the thighes are also spottet with whitte. He hath a chayne abowt his necke of white beades, betweene which are other Rownde beades of copper which they esteeme more then golde or silver. This Idol is placed in the temple of the towne of Secotam, as the keper of the kings dead corpses. Somtyme they have two of thes idoles in theyr churches, and sometinez, but never above, which they place in a darke corner wher they shew terrible. Thes poore soules have none other knowledge of god although I thinke them verye Desirous to know the truthe. For when as wee kneeled downe on our knees to make our prayers unto god, they went abowt to imitate us, and when they saw we moved our lipps, they also dyd the like. Wherfore that is verye like that they might easelye be brongt[3] to the knowledge of the gospel. God of his mercie grant them this grace.

[3] Brought.

XXII.

The Tombe of their Werovvans
or Cheiff Lordes.

he builde a Scaffolde 9. or 10. foote hihe as is expressed in this figure under the tombs of their Weroans, or cheefe lordes which they cover with matts, and lai the dead corpses of their weroans theruppon in manner followinge. first the bowells are taken forthe. Then layinge downe the skinne, they cutt all the flesh cleane from the bones, which the drye in the sonne, and well dryed the inclose in Matts, and place at their feete. Then their bones (remaininge still fastened together with the ligaments whole and uncorrupted) are covered a gayne with leather, and their carcase fashioned as yf their flesh wear not taken away. They lapp eache corps in his owne skinne after the same is thus handled, and lay yt in his order by the corpses of the other cheef lordes. By the dead bodies they sett their Idol Kiwasa. . . . For they are persuaded that the same doth kepe the dead bodyes of their cheefe lordes that nothinge may hurt them. Moreover under the foresaid scaffolde some on[1] of their preists hath his lodginge, which Mumbleth his prayers nighte and day, and hath charge of the corpses. For his bedd he hath two deares skinnes spredd on the grownde, yf the wether bee cold hee maketh a fyre to warme by withall. Thes poore soules are thus instructed by nature to reverence their princes even after their death.

[1] One.

Ther Idol Kivvafa.   XXI.

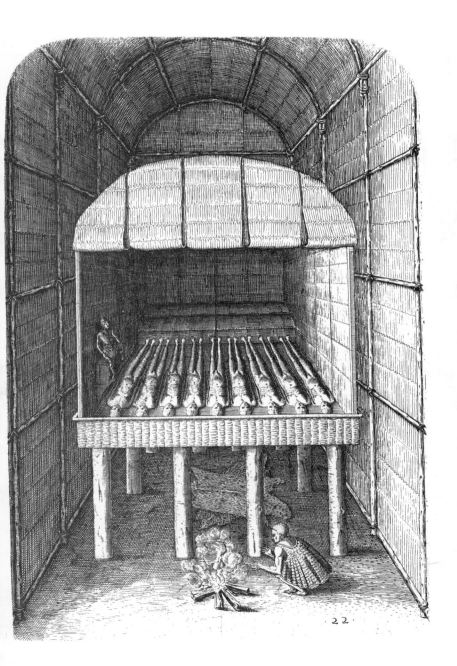

22

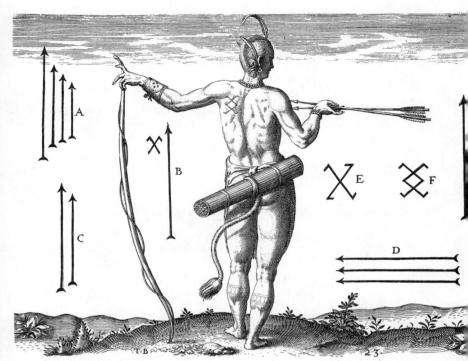

he inhabitants of all the cuntrie for the most parte have marks rased on their backs, wherby yt may be knowen what Princes subjects they bee, or of what place they have their originall.[1] For which cause we have set downe those marks in this figure. . . . that they might more easelye be discerned. Which industrie hath god indued[2] them withal although they be verye sinple, and rude. And to confesse a truthe I cannot remember, that ever I saw a better or quietter people then they.

The marks which I observed amonge them, are heere put downe in order folowinge.

The marke which is expressed by A. belongeth tho Wingino, the cheefe lorde of Roanoac.

That which hath B. is the marke of Wingino his sisters husbande.

Those which be noted with the letters, of C. and D. belonge unto diverse chefe lordes in Secotam.

Those which have the letters E. F. G. are certaine cheefe men
of Pomeiooc, and Aquascogoc.

[1] Origins. [2] Endued, bestowed.

102

SOM PICTVRE,
OF THE PICTES
WHICH IN THE OLDE
tyme dyd habite one part of the
great Bretainne.

THE PAINTER OF WHOM I HAVE
had the firſt of the Inhabitans of Uirginia, giue my allſo thees 5. Figures
fallowinge, fownd as hy did aſſured my in a oolld English cronicle, the which
I wold well ſett to the ende of thees firſt Figures, for to showe how that
the Inhabitants of the great Bretannie haue bin in ti-
mes paſt as ſauuage as thoſe of
Uirginia.

E

T · B · J ·

The trvve picture of one
Picte I.

n tymes past the Pictes, habitans of one part of great Bretainne, which is nowe nammed England, wear savvages, and did paint all their bodye after the maner followinge, the did lett their haire growe as fare as their Shoulders, savinge those which hange uppon their forehead, the which the did cutt. They shave all their berde except the mustaches, uppon their breast wear painted the head of som birde, ant about the pappes[1] as yt waere beames of the sune, uppon the bellye sum feerefull and monstreus face, spreedinge the beames verye fare uppon the thighes. Upon the tow knees som faces of lion, and uppon their leggs as yt hath been shelles of fish. Upon their Shoulders griffones heades, and then they hath serpents abowt their armes: They caried abowt their necks one ayerne[2] ringe, and another abowt the midds of their bodye, abowt the bellye, and the saids hange on a chaine, a cimeterre or turkie soorde,[3] the did carye in one arme a target[4] made of wode, and in the other hande a picke, of which the ayerne was after the manner of a Lick,[5] whith tassels on, and the other ende with a Rounde boule.[6] And when they hath overcomme some of their ennemis, they did never felle[7] to carye a we their heads with them.

[1] Nipples. [2] Iron. [3] Scimitar or Turkish sword, a sword with a curved blade. [4] Small shield. [5] Spear-shaped. [6] Bowl. [7] Fail.

The trvve picture of a vvomen
Picte II.

he woemen of the Pictes above said wear noe worser for the warres then the men. And wear paynted after the manner followinge, havinge their heads bear, did lett their hairre flyinge. abowt their Showlders wear painted with griffon heades, the lowe parts and thighes with lion faces, or some other beaste as yt commeth best into their fansye, their brest hath a maner of a half moone, with a great stare,[8] and fowre lesser[9] in booth the sides, their pappes[10] painted in maner of beames of the sonne, and among all this a great litteninge[11] starre uppon their brests. The saids of som pointes or beames, and the hoolle bellye as a sonne, the armes, thighes, and leggs well painted, of diverses Figures: The dyd also carye abowt theyr necks an ayern[12] Ringe, as the men did, and suche a girdle with the soorde hainginge, havinge a Picke or a lance in one hande, and twoe dardz[13] in the other.

[8] Star. [9] Four lesser, i.e., four smaller stars. [10] Nipples. [11] Glistening. [12] Iron. [13] Darts.

T·B 2

5

SIR WALTER RALEGH

"Of the Voyage for Guiana"
1596?

Sir Walter Ralegh (1552?–1618) was the most prominent Englishman who tried to create English colonies in North America. A close ally of Queen Elizabeth, he had received from her a patent to territory along the east coast of North America, including Roanoke Island off the coast of present-day North Carolina. But by the end of the sixteenth century, he was concentrating his efforts on establishing a colony in Guiana, a region in northern South America surrounded by Spanish territory. Like the Spanish, who believed that colonies would produce mineral wealth for Europeans, Ralegh thought that the English would find gold and silver in Guiana. To press his case and to encourage continued English efforts to colonize central America, he published a book entitled The Discoverie of the Large, Rich, and Beautiful Empire of Guiana *in 1596. At approximately the same time, he wrote "Of the Voyage for Guiana."*

Apparently in Ralegh's hand (and not published at the time), the tract contains a brief overview of Ralegh's plans for the colony and is consistent with the material presented in the much longer Discoverie. *Here he emphasized the religious benefits of colonizing Guiana, the wealth that the nation would gain from such a venture, and the advantage that the colony would have in England's ceaseless competition with Spain. Like other authors, Ralegh cited biblical authorities to justify the venture, with references to the books of Genesis, Daniel, Judges 2, and Luke among others.*

In the end, Ralegh's propagandizing failed. The English could not colonize Guiana with any success. Many of the people who accompanied Ralegh to Guiana lost their lives in a venture there in 1618, and Ralegh did not find the mineral wealth he sought. Ralegh never gave up trying to establish an English presence in Guiana, but his failure to do so made him vulnerable to the hostility of James I (reigned 1603–1625), who did not share Elizabeth's

---

Sir Walter Ralegh, "Of the Voyage for Guiana," in Robert H. Schomburgk, ed., *The Discovery of the Large, Rich, and Beautiful Empire of Guiana . . . by Sir. W. Ralegh,* Works Issued by the Hakluyt Society, no. 3 (n.d.; reprint, New York: Burt Franklin, 1970), 135–53.

animosity toward the Spanish. In an effort to appease the Spanish King Philip III, who despised Ralegh's efforts to establish an English presence in Guiana, James ordered Ralegh beheaded shortly after his return from the 1618 voyage.

What are Ralegh's arguments in favor of colonizing Guiana? Which arguments do you think would have been most persuasive to the English monarch and government? To potential emigrants? Why does Ralegh argue that Guiana would have a special role in the English colonial empire? What does the tone of Ralegh's work suggest about English attitudes toward Spain at the end of the sixteenth century?

Touching the voyage for Guiana it is to be considered first, whether it bee to be undertaken: secondly, the manner of subduing it: and lastly, the meanes howe to subdue it, and annex it to the Crowne Imperiall of the Realme of England.

That it is to be undertaken will appeare, if it be proved to bee (1) honorable, (2) profitable, (3) necessary, (4) and with no greate chardge, or difficultye accomplished.

1. It is honorable, both for that by this meanes infinite nombers of soules may be brought from theyr idolatry, bloody sacrifices, ignoraunce, and incivility to the worshipping of the true God aright to civill conversation, and also theyr bodyes freed from the intollerable tirrany of the Spaniards whereunto they are already or likely in shorte space to bee subjected, unlesse her excellent Majestie or some other christian prince doe speedily assiste, and afterward protect them in their just defensive wars against the violence of usurpers which if it please her highnes to undertake, besids that presently it will stopp the mouthes of the Romish Catholickes, who vaunt[1] of theyr great adventures for the propogacion of the gospell,[2] it will add greate increase of honor, to the memory of her Majesties name upon earth to all posterity and in the end bee rewarded with an excellent starlike splendency in the heavens, which is reserved for them that turne many unto righteousnes, as the Prophet speaketh.

2. Likewise it is profitable, for heereby the Queens dominions may bee exceedingly enlarged, and this Realme inestimably enriched, with pretious stones, gold, silver, pearle, and other commodityes which those countryes yeald, and (God giving good successe to the voyage) an entrance

---

[1] Boast.
[2] The desire to spread Catholicism constituted a major component of the colonizing ventures of the Spanish, Portuguese, and French.

made thereby to many other Empyres, (which hapily may prove as rich as this) and it may bee to Peru it selfe and other Kingdomes of which the Spaniards bee now possessed, in those partes and else where.

3. Lastly, the necessity of attempting Guiana in regard of our owne security (albeit noe profite should redound thereby to the Indians, or to ourselves directly from those countryes) ought greatly to weigh with us. For if the Spaniards by the treasure of those Kingdomes which hee hath already, be able to trouble the better parte of Christendome, what would hee doe if hee were once established in Guiana, which is thought to bee more rich then all other lands which hee enjoyeth either in the East or West Indies. Whereas if her Majestie weare seased[3] of it, hee mighte bee soe kepte occupied in those provinces that hee would not hastely threaten us, with any more of his invincible navies.

But although this voyage were never so honorable, profitable, or necessary for our estate to be undertaken, yet if we had not some possibility for the effecting of our purpose, it were more meete to strengthen our selves at home, then to weaken our forces in seeking to annoy our enemy abroad. But such opportunity and so many encourage- ments doe now offer themselves unto her highnes that (I suppose) there is no prince in the world but hee would greatly strayne hymselfe, rather then to omitt the advantage of such a booty. Among others, these inducements are to bee weighed.

1. The Bordurers,[4] who are sayd to bee naturalls,[5] and to whom onely the Empire of Guiana doth of right apperteine,[6] are already prepared to joyne with us, having submitted themselves to the Queen's protection both against the Spaniards and Emperor of Guiana who usurpeth upon them.

2. The Spaniards for theyr oppressions and usurpations, are detested and feared both by the Guianians and bordurers, by the former, beecause the Spaniards forced them to fly from theyr owne country of Peru, and by the latter, by experience of the Spanish dealing towardes themselves and theyr adjoyning neighbors. So as it is reported none doe assiste them save the Arwacans, a vagabond, poore, and small people. But it is like[7] that all the countryes of the continent who are not yet inthralled to the Spaniards

---

[3] Seized.
[4] Those dwelling outside Guiana in adjoining territory (i.e., at the borders).
[5] Natives; i.e., Indians.
[6] Belong.
[7] Likely.

and have heard of their outrage and especially the Amazones[8] in regarde of their sexe, will be ready to ayd her Majestie against the Spaniards.

3. The voyage is shorte being but 6 weekes sayling from England and the like backe againe, which may so bee contrived as going, abiding, and returning we may bestow[9] an whole yeare without any winter at all by the way, no lee shore, no sandes, or enimies coast.

4. No chardge but onely at the first setting forth which need not be great, especially if the course layd downe in this treatise of some such like, be taken, considering the country yeeldeth store of corne, beasts, fowle, fish and fruit for victualls,[10] and steele and copper for the making of armor and ordinance,[11] and among the Amapagotos and Caraccas horses may be had and in short time manned for our service in the wars.

5. It is thought the passage to it may bee easely fortifyed by sea and the country by nature is defensed by land with mountaines and multitude of nations, that it is impossible in manner by land to bee evicted, beeing once attayned by us.

6. Though we are not greatly to rely upon prophesies, yet if it weare found in Peru (as Don Anthonio de Berreo[12] told Sir Walter Ralegh) among other prophesies that from Inglatiera[13] the Inga[14] should be restored to Peru, it may fall out to bee true (as many of theyr prophesies did both in Mexico and Peru which indeed foreshewed the altaration of those Empires) at least the prophesy will greatly daunt the Spaniards[15] and make them afrayd of the worst event in these imployments.

7. If it be remembred how the Spaniards have without just title or any wrong at all donne to them by the harmelesse Indians, forceably envaded and wrongfully deteyned their countryes aboute 100 yeares, committing barbarous and exquisite[16] massacres to the distruction of whole nations of people (arising by estimacion of some of accompt[17] among them and acquaynted with theyr proceedings in some few yeares to the number of 20 millions of reasonable creatures made to the Image of God and lesse harmefull then the Spaniards themselves) whereby more fruitfull land was

---

[8] The group of female warriors found in South America by the Spanish, named by them after the Amazons of Greek mythology.

[9] Devote.

[10] Food or provisions.

[11] Ordinance; i.e., weapons.

[12] Dom Antonio (1531–1595), pretender to the Portuguese crown, supported in some of his naval expeditions by England.

[13] At the hands of the English.

[14] Incas.

[15] The fear of the Incas regaining their territory would make the Spanish apprehensive.

[16] Excruciatingly painful.

[17] Account.

layd wast and depopulated then is in all Europe and some parte of Asia, in revenge wherof their owne religious men do make accompte that the just God in judgment will one day horribly chasten and peradventure wholy subvert and root out the Spanish nation from the world. Againe if it bee noted that the Spaniards have above 20 severall times in vayne sought the conquest of Guiana, and that it doth by the providence of the Almighty now (as it were) prostrate herselfe before her Majesties feet the most potent enemy that the Spaniards hath, not onely intreating but by unvaluable offers and unanswerable reasons alluring, even urging and forcing her highnes to accept it under her alleigeaunce, who would not bee perswaded that now at length the great judge of the world, hath heard the sighes, grones, lamentacions, teares, and bloud of so many millions of innocent men, women, and children aflicted, robbed, reviled, branded with hot irons, roasted, dismembred, mangled, stabbed, whipped, racked, scalded with hott oyle, suet,[18] and hogsgrease, put to the strapado,[19] ripped alive, beheaded in sport, drowned, dashd against the rocks, famished, devoured by mastifes,[20] burned and by infinite crueltyes consumed, and purposeth to scourge and plague that cursed nation, and to take the yoake of servitude from that distressed people, as free by nature as any Christian. In comtemplacion of all which things, who would not bee incouraged to proceed in this voyage, having in a maner none other enemyes but these Spaniards, abhorred of God, and man, being provoked by so many allurements, occacions, reasons, and opportunityes, in a most just cause, the safety of our dread soveraigne, of our selves, and of a great part of the Christian world thereuppon depending.

[18] Animal fat used in cooking and candle making.
[19] Strappado, a form of torture devised to extract a confession. The victim's hands were tied behind his or her back and fastened to a pulley; the victim was then lifted up from the ground and let down halfway, stopping with a jerk to maximize the pain.
[20] Mastiffs, large dogs.

6

GEORGE PERCY

"A Discourse of the Plantation
of the Southern Colonie in Virginia"
1606–1607

Amidst all the celebratory tracts that the promoters issued about the great
opportunities available to the English in North America, George Percy's "A
Discourse of the Plantation of the Southern Colonie in Virginia" was surely
a departure. Percy (1580–1632) was among the first colonists sent by the
Virginia Company to settle at Jamestown in the territory the English termed
"Virginia." Instead of dwelling on the great resources available in America
(though he wrote about them in his "Discourse"), the account left by Percy
revealed the human costs of settlement schemes, notably the deaths of many
colonists in Jamestown during the summer of 1607. But in spite of its catalog
of suffering, Percy's tract also revealed the descriptive talents of a perceptive
observer of early English colonization efforts.

Percy's account, apparently based on a diary he kept from December 1606
to September 1607, was published in London in 1625 in a collection edited by
Samuel Purchas, who was carrying on the work of Richard Hakluyt the
younger by compiling travel accounts. Percy's account appeared in Purchas's
four-volume collection of travel writing entitled Hakluytus Posthumus or
Purchas His Pilgrimes. Though Purchas did not print all of Percy's diary,
the richness of the text suggests that he did not edit it to serve any particular
purpose. Instead, Purchas presumably saw in Percy's account a realistic
assessment of the opportunities and dangers awaiting any English man or
woman who wanted to travel to America.

By including observations of his travels through the West Indies before
reaching Virginia, Percy's "Discourse" revealed that migration abroad was
not a simple process of leaving an English port and disembarking in
Virginia. Instead, Percy and his shipmates had to negotiate with various
groups of Indians, some of whom he believed practiced cannibalism. As
would become increasingly evident in travel accounts, Percy learned how to

---

George Percy, "A Discourse of the Plantation of the Southern Colonie in Virginia," in David
Beers Quinn and Alison O. Quinn, eds. New American World, 5 vols. (New York and
London: Macmillan, 1979), 5:266–74.

draw distinctions between Indian groups and recognized the importance of negotiating with those who could dispense the greatest help to the struggling colonists at Jamestown.

Percy was hardly a representative colonist. As the eighth son of Henry Percy, the eighth earl of Northumberland, Percy no doubt held views different from many of the poorer migrants to North America. For Percy and other members of elite families, particularly younger sons who could not inherit their fathers' estates because of English rules of primogeniture and entail (which required that landed estates be passed on intact to the eldest son), colonization ventures seemed a possible road to the wealth they desperately wanted but could not obtain in England. Percy's status enabled him to become one of the earliest leaders of the Virginia Company; he served a brief stint as Jamestown's deputy governor before he returned to England in 1612. Percy did not always agree with the management of the colony, and he did not get along too well with Virginia's most prominent leader, Captain John Smith.

In what ways could Percy's role in Virginia have influenced his "Discourse"? Does the tract contain the same promotional tone as the work of others, such as the Hakluyts? How are Percy's descriptions of the Indians similar to and different from those of Harriot and White? If his report had been published when it was written, what impact do you think it could have had on potential migrants? Why, given the apparent risks, did many continue to migrate to Virginia even after the publication of this account in 1625?

On Saturday the twentieth of December in the yeere 1606. the fleet fell from London, and the fift of January we anchored in the Downes;[1] but the winds continued contrarie so long, that we were forced to stay there some time, where wee suffered great stormes, but by the skilfulnesse of the Captaine wee suffered no great losse or danger.

The twelfth day of February at night we saw a blazing Starre, and presently a storme. The three and twentieth day we fell with the Iland of Mattanenio[2] in the West Indies. The foure and twentieth day we anchored at Dominico,[3] within fourteene degrees of the Line,[4] a very faire Iland, the Trees full of sweet and good smels inhabited by many Savage Indians, they

[1] The Downs, a roadstead (that is, a place in the open sea where ships can safely anchor) at the eastern end of the English Channel.
[2] Probably Martinique.
[3] Dominica, a small island just northwest of Martinique.
[4] The equator.

were at first very scrupulous[5] to come aboord us. Wee learned of them afterwards that the Spaniards had given them a great overthrow on this Ile, but when they knew what we were, there came many to our ships with their Canoas, bringing us many kindes of sundry fruites, as Pines, Potatoes, Plantons,[6] Tobacco, and other fruits, and Roane Cloth[7] abundance, which they had gotten out of certaine Spanish ships that were cast away upon that Iland. We gave them Knives, Hatchets for exchange which they esteeme much, wee also gave them Beades, Copper Jewels which they hang through their nosthrils, eares, and lips, very strange to behold, their bodies are all painted red to keepe away the biting of Muscetos, they goe all naked without covering: the haire of their head is a yard long, all of a length pleated in three plats[8] hanging downe to their wastes, they suffer no haire to grow on their faces, they cut their skinnes in divers workes,[9] they are continually in warres, and will eate their enemies when they kill them, or any stranger if they take them. They will lap up mans spittle, whilst one spits in their mouthes in a barbarous fashion like Dogges. These people and the rest of the Ilands in the West Indies, and Brasill, are called by the names of Canibals, that will eate mans flesh, these people doe poyson their Arrow heads, which are made of a fishes bone: they worship the Devill for their God, and have no other beliefe. Whilest we remayned at this Iland we saw a Whale chased by a Thresher[10] and a Swordfish: they fought for the space of two houres, we might see the Thresher with his flayle lay on the monstrous blowes which was strange to behold: in the end these two fishes brought the Whale to her end.

The sixe and twentieth day, we had sight of Marigalanta,[11] and the next day wee sailed with a slacke saile alongst the Ile of Guadulupa,[12] where we went ashore, and found a Bath which was so hot, that no man was able to stand long by it, our Admirall Captaine Newport caused a piece of Porke to be put in it: which boyled it so in the space of halfe an houre, as no fire could mend it. Then we went aboord and sailed by many Ilands, as Mounserot[13] and an Iland called Saint Christopher, both uninhabited about; about two a clocke in the afternoone wee anchored at the Ile of Mevis.[14] There the Captaine landed all his men being well fitted with

[5] Cautious, reluctant.
[6] Pines are pineapples; plantons are plantains, bananalike fruit indigenous to the tropics.
[7] Roan cloth, a linen made in Rouen, France, traded at the time.
[8] Braided in three braids.
[9] Ornamental patterns.
[10] A type of shark.
[11] Marie-Galante, a small island north of Dominica.
[12] Guadeloupe, a larger island northwest of Marie-Galante.
[13] Montserrat, northwest of Guadeloupe.
[14] Nevis, a small island between Montserrat and St. Christopher (St. Kitts).

Muskets and other convenient Armes, marched a mile into the Woods; being commanded to stand upon their guard, fearing the treacherie of the Indians, which is an ordinary use amongst them and all other Savages on this Ile, we came to a Bath standing in a Valley betwixt two Hils; where wee bathed our selves and found it to be of the nature of the Bathes in England, some places hot and some colder: and men may refresh themselves as they please, finding this place to be so convenient for our men to avoid diseases, which will breed in so long a Voyage, wee incamped our selves on this Ile six dayes, and spent none of our ships victuall,[15] by reason our men some went a hunting, some a fouling, and some a fishing, where we got great store of Conies,[16] sundry kinds of fowles, and great plentie of fish. We kept Centinels and Courts de gard[17] at every Captaines quarter, fearing wee should be assaulted by the Indians, that were on the other side of the Iland: wee saw none nor were molested by any: but some few we saw as we were a hunting on the Iland. They would not come to us by any meanes, but ranne swiftly through the Woods to the Mountaine tops; so we lost the sight of them: whereupon we made all the haste wee could to our quarter, thinking there had beene a great ambush of Indians there abouts. We past into the thickest of the Woods where we had almost lost our selves, we had not gone above halfe a mile amongst the thicke, but we came into a most pleasant Garden, being a hundred paces square on every side, having many Cotton-trees growing in it with abundance of Cotton-wooll, and many Guiacum[18] trees: wee saw the goodliest tall trees growing so thicke about the Garden, as though they had beene set by Art, which made us marvell very much to see it.

The third day, wee set saile from Mevis: the fourth day we sailed along by Castutia[19] and by Saba: This day we anchored at the Ile of Virgines, in an excellent Bay able to harbour a hundred Ships: if this Bay stood in England, it would be a great profit and commoditie to the Land. On this Iland wee caught great store of Fresh-fish, and abundance of Sea Tortoises, which served all our Fleet three daies, which were in number eight score persons. We also killed great store of wilde Fowle, wee cut the Barkes of certaine Trees which tasted much like Cinnamon, and very hot in the mouth. This Iland in some places hath very good ground, straight and tall Timber. But the greatest discommoditie that wee have seene on

---

[15] Food or provisions.
[16] Rabbits.
[17] On guard.
[18] Guaiacum, a type of tree and shrub native to the West Indies and tropical parts of America.
[19] Probably St. Eustatius, which lies between St. Kitts and Saba.

this Iland is that it hath no Fresh-water, which makes the place void of any Inhabitants.

Upon the sixt day, we set saile and passed by Becam,[20] and by Saint John de Porto Rico. The seventh day, we arrived at Mona.[21] where wee watered, which we stood in great need of, seeing that our water did smell so vildly that none of our men were able to indure it. Whilst some of the Saylers were a filling the Caskes with water, the Captaine, and the rest of the Gentlemen, and other Soldiers marched up in the Ile sixe myles, thinking to find some other provision to maintaine our victualling; as wee marched we killed two wild Bores, and saw a huge wild Bull, his hornes was an ell betweene the two tops. Wee also killed Guanas,[22] in fashion of a Serpent, and speckled like a Toade under the belly. These wayes that wee went, being so troublesome and vilde going upon the sharpe Rockes, that many of our men fainted in the march, but by good fortune wee lost none but one Edward Brookes Gentleman, whose fat melted within him by the great heate and drought of the Countrey: we were not able to relieve him nor our selves, so he died in that great extreamitie.

The ninth day in the afternoone, we went off with our Boat to the Ile of Moneta,[23] some three leagues from Mona, where we had a terrible landing, and a troublesome getting up to the top of the Mountaine or Ile, being a high firme Rocke step, with many terrible sharpe stones: After wee got to the top of the Ile, we found it to bee a fertill and a plaine ground, full of goodly grasse, and abundance of Fowles of all kindes, they flew over our heads as thicke as drops of Hale; besides they made such a noise, that wee were not able to heare one another speake. Furthermore, wee were not able to set our feet on the ground, but either on Fowles or Egges which lay so thicke in the grasse: Wee laded two Boats full in the space of three houres, to our great refreshing.

The tenth day we set saile, and disimboged[24] out of the West Indies, and bare our course Northerly. The fourteenth day we passed the Tropicke of Cancer. The one and twentieth day, about five a clocke at night there began a vehement tempest, which lasted all the night, with winds, raine, and thunders in a terrible manner. Wee were forced to lie at Hull[25] that night, because we thought wee had beene neerer land then wee were. The next morning, being the two and twentieth day wee sounded; and the three and twentieth and foure and twentieth day, but we could find no

---

[20] Possibly Vieques, a small island just east of Puerto Rico.
[21] Mona Island, off the western coast of Puerto Rico.
[22] Iguanas.
[23] Monito, a tiny island northwest of Mona.
[24] Disembogued, sailed out into the open sea.
[25] To drift with the wind with sails furled.

ground. The five and twentieth day we sounded, and had no ground at an hundred fathom. The six and twentieth day of Aprill, about foure a clocke in the morning, wee descried[26] the Land of Virginia: the same day wee entred into the Bay of Chesupioc[27] directly, without any let or hinderance; there wee landed and discovered[28] a little way, but wee could find nothing worth the speaking of, but faire meddowes and goodly tall Trees, with such Fresh-waters running through the woods, as I was almost ravished at the first sight thereof.

At night, when wee were going aboard, there came the Savages creeping upon all foure, from the Hills like Beares, with their Bowes in their mouthes, charged us very desperately in the faces, hurt Captaine Gabrill Archer in both his hands, and a sayler in two places of the body very dangerous. After they had spent their Arrowes, and felt the sharpnesse of our shot, they retired into the Woods with a great noise, and so left us.

The seven and twentieth day we began to build up our Shallop:[29] the Gentlemen and Souldiers marched eight miles up into the Land, we could not see a Savage in all that march, we came to a place where they had made a great fire, and had beene newly a rosting Oysters: when they perceived our comming, they fled away to the Mountaines, and left many of the Oysters in the fire: we eat some of the Oysters, which were very large and delicate in taste.

The eighteenth day we lanched our Shallop, the Captaine and some Gentlemen went in her, and discovered up the Bay, we found a River on the Southside running into the Maine;[30] we entered it and found it very shoald[31] water, not for any Boats to swim: Wee went further into the Bay, and saw a plaine plot of ground where we went on Land, and found the place five mile in compasse, without either Bush or Tree, we saw nothing there but a Cannow, which was made out of the whole tree, which was five and fortie foot long by the Rule. Upon this plot of ground we got good store of Mussels and Oysters, which lay on the ground as thicke as stones: wee opened some, and found in many of them Pearles. Wee marched some three or foure miles further into the Woods, where we saw great smoakes of fire. Wee marched to those smoakes and found that the Savages had beene there burning downe the grasse, as wee thought either to make their plantation there, or else to give signes to bring their forces

[26] Discovered, caught sight of.
[27] Chesapeake.
[28] Reconnoitered, explored.
[29] A small boat or sloop used mainly in shallow water.
[30] Mainland.
[31] Shallow.

together, and so to give us battell. We past through excellent ground full of Flowers of divers kinds and colours, and as goodly trees as I have seene, as Cedar, Cipresse, and other kindes: going a little further we came into a little plat of ground full of fine and beautifull Strawberries, foure times bigger and better then ours in England. All this march we could neither see Savage nor Towne. When it grew to be towards night we stood backe to our Ships, we sounded and found it shallow water for a great way, which put us out of all hopes for getting any higher with our Ships, which road at the mouth of the River. Wee rowed over to a point of Land, where wee found a channell, and sounded six, eight, ten, or twelve fathom: which put us in good comfort. Therefore wee named that point of Land, Cape Comfort.

The nine and twentieth day we set up a Crosse at Chesupioc Bay, and named that place Cape Henry. Thirtieth day, we came with our ships to Cape Comfort; where wee saw five Savages running on the shoare; presently the Captaine caused the shallop to be manned, so rowing to the shoare, the Captaine called to them in signe of friendship, but they were at first very timersome,[32] until they saw the Captain lay his hand on his heart: upon that they laid down their Bowes and Arrowes, and came very boldly to us, making signes to come to shoare to their Towne, which is called by the Savages Kecoughtan. Wee coasted to their Towne, rowing over a River running into the Maine, where these Savages swam over with their Bowes and Arrowes in their mouthes.

When we came over to the other side, there was a many of other Savages which directed us to their Towne, where we were entertained by them very kindly. When we came first a Land they made a dolefull noise, laying their faces to the ground, scratching the earth with their nailes. We did thinke that they had beene at their Idolatry. When they had ended their Ceremonies, they went into their houses and brought out mats and laid upon the ground, the chiefest of them sate all in a rank: the meanest[33] sort brought us such dainties as they had, & of their bread which they make of their Maiz or Gennea wheat,[34] they would not suffer us to eat unlesse we sate down, which we did on a Mat right against them. After we were well satisfied they gave us of their Tabacco, which they tooke in a pipe made artificially of earth as ours are, but far bigger, with the bowle fashioned together with a piece of fine copper. After they had feasted us, they shewed us, in welcome, their manner of dancing, which was in this fashion: one of the Savages standing in the midst singing, beating one hand

---

[32] Timorous, fearful.
[33] Lowest in rank.
[34] Maize and guinea wheat are both types of Indian corn.

against another, all the rest dancing about him, shouting, howling, and stamping against the ground, with many Anticke[35] tricks and faces, making noise like so many Wolves or Devils. One thing of them I observed; when they were in their dance they kept stroke with their feet just one with another, but with their hands, heads, faces, and bodies, every one of them had a severall gesture: so they continued for the space of halfe an houre. When they had ended their dance, the Captaine gave them Beades and other trifling Jewells. They hang through their eares Fowles legs: they shave the right side of their heads with a shell, the left side they weare of an ell long tied up with an artificiall knot, with a many of Foules feathers sticking in it. They goe altogether naked, but their privities are covered with Beasts skinnes beset commonly with little bones, or beasts teeth: some paint their bodies blacke, some red, with artificiall knots of sundry lively colours, very beautifull and pleasing to the eye, in a braver fashion then they in the West Indies.

The fourth day of May, we came to the King of Werowance[36] of Paspihe: where they entertained us with much welcome; an old Savage made a long Oration, making a foule noise, uttering his speech with a vehement action, but we knew little what they meant. Whilst we were in company with the Paspihes, the Werowance of Rapahanna came from the other side of the River in his Cannoa: he seemed to take displeasure of our being with the Paspihes: he would faine[37] have had us come to his Towne, the Captaine was unwilling; seeing that the day was so far spent he returned backe to his ships for that night.

The next day, being the fift of May, the Werowance of Rapahanna sent a Messenger to have us come to him. We entertained the said Messenger, and gave him trifles which pleased him: Wee manned our shallop with Muskets and Targatiers[38] sufficiently: this said Messenger guided us where our determination was to goe. When wee landed, the Werowance of Rapahanna came downe to the water side with all his traine, as goodly men as any I have seene of Savages or Christians: the Werowance comming before them playing on a Flute made of a Reed, with a Crown of Deares haire colloured red, in fashion of a Rose fastened about his knot of haire, and a great Plate of Copper on the other side of his head, with two long Feathers in fashion of a paire of Hornes placed in the midst of his Crowne. His body was painted all with

---

[35] Antic, grotesque or bizarre.

[36] Indian chief. The Paspaheghs and Rappahannocks were tribes in the Chesapeake region. For the location of the Paspaheghs and Rappahannocks, see Helen C. Rountree, *Pocahontas's People: The Powhatan Indians of Virginia through Four Centuries* (Norman: University of Oklahoma Press, 1990), 11.

[37] Fain, gladly.

[38] Targeteers, foot soldiers armed with shields.

Crimson, with a Chaine of Beads about his necke, his face painted blew, besprinkled with silver Ore as wee thought, his eares all behung with Braslets of Pearle, and in either eare a Birds Claw through it beset with fine Copper or Gold, he entertained us in so modest a proud fashion, as though he had beene a Prince of civill government, holding his countenance without laughter or any such ill behaviour; he caused his Mat to be spred on the ground, where hee sate downe with a great Majestie, taking a pipe of Tabacco: the rest of his company standing about him. After he had rested a while he rose, and made signes to us to come to his Towne: Hee went formost, and all the rest of his people and our selves followed him up a steepe Hill where his Palace was settled. Wee passed through the Woods in fine paths, having most pleasant Springs which issued from the Mountaines: Wee also went through the goodliest Corne fieldes that ever was seene in any Countrey. When wee came to Rapahannos Towne, hee entertained us in good humanitie.

The eight day of May we discovered up the River. We landed in the Countrey of Apamatica,[39] at our landing, there came many stout and able Savages to resist us with their Bowes and Arrowes, in a most warlike manner, with the swords at their backes beset with sharpe stones, and pieces of yron able to cleave a man in sunder. Amongst the rest one of the chiefest standing before them crosse-legged, with his Arrow readie in his Bow in one hand, and taking a Pipe of Tobacco in the other, with a bold uttering of his speech, demanded of us our being there, willing us to bee gone. Wee made signes of peace, which they perceived in the end, and let us land in quietnesse.

The twelfth day we went backe to our ships, and discovered a point of Land, called Archers Hope, which was sufficient with a little labour to defend our selves against any Enemy. The soile was good and fruitfull, with excellent good Timber. There are also great store of Vines in bignesse of a mans thigh, running up to the tops of the Trees in great abundance. We also did see many Squirels, Conies, Black Birds with crimson wings, and divers other Fowles and Birds of divers and sundrie collours of Crimson, Watchet,[40] Yellow, Greene, Murry,[41] and of divers other hewes naturally without any art using.

We found store of Turkie nests and many Egges, if it had not beene disliked, because the ship could not ride neere the shoare, we had setled there to all the Collonies contentment.

The thirteenth day, we came to our seating place in Paspihas Countrey,

---

[39] Appomattox.
[40] Light blue.
[41] Murrey, purple-red, the color of mulberry.

some eight miles from the point of Land, which I made mention before: where our shippes doe lie so neere the shoare that they are moored to the Trees in six fathom water.

The fourteenth day we landed all our men which were set to worke about the fortification, and others some to watch and ward as it was convenient. The first night of our landing, about midnight, there came some Savages sayling close to our quarter: presently there was an alarum given; upon that the Savages ran away, and we not troubled any more by them that night. Not long after there came two Savages that seemed to be Commanders, bravely drest, with Crownes of coloured haire upon their heads, which came as Messengers from the Werowance of Paspiha; telling us that their Werowance was comming and would be merry with us with a fat Deare.

The eighteenth day, the Werowance of Paspiha came himselfe to our quarter, with one hundred Savages armed, which garded him in a very warlike manner with Bowes and Arrowes, thinking at that time to execute their villany. Paspiha made great signes to us to lay our Armes away. But we would not trust him so far: he seeing he could not have convenient time to worke his will, at length made signes that he would give us as much land as we would desire to take. As the Savages were in a throng in the Fort, one of them stole a Hatchet from one of our company, which spied him doing the deed: whereupon he tooke it from him by force, and also strooke him over the arme: presently another Savage seeing that, came fiercely at our man with a wooden sword, thinking to beat out his braines. The Werowance of Paspiha saw us take to our Armes, went suddenly away with all his company in great anger.

The nineteenth day, my selfe and three or foure more walking into the Woods by chance wee espied a path-way like to an Irish pace:[42] wee were desirous to knowe whither it would bring us; wee traced along some foure miles, all the way as wee went, having the pleasantest Suckles,[43] the ground all flowing over with faire flowers of sundry colours and kindes, as though it had beene in any Garden or Orchard in England. There be many Strawberries, and other fruits unknowne: wee saw the Woods full of Cedar and Cypresse trees, with other trees, which issues out sweet Gummes like to Balsam: wee kept on our way in this Paradise, at length wee came to a Savage Towne, where wee found but few people, they told us the rest were gone a hunting with the Werowance of Paspiha: we stayed there a while, and had of them Strawberries, and other things; in

---

[42] A narrow passage between woods or the like, presumably as in Ireland.
[43] Honeysuckles.

the meane time one of the Savages came running out of his house with a Bowe and Arrowes and ranne mainly through the Woods: then I beganne to mistrust some villanie, that he went to call some companie, and so betray us, wee made all the haste away wee could: one of the Savages brought us on the way to the Wood side, where there was a Garden of Tobacco, and other fruits and herbes, he gathered Tobacco, and distributed to every one of us, so wee departed.

The twentieth day the Werowance of Paspiha sent fortie of his men with a Deere, to our quarter: but they came more in villanie than any love they bare us: they faine would have layne in our Fort all night, but wee would not suffer them for feare of their treachery. One of our Gentlemen having a Target[44] which hee trusted in, thinking it would beare out a slight shot, hee set it up against a tree, willing one of the Savages to shoot; who tooke from his backe an Arrow of an elle long,[45] drew it strongly in his Bowe, shoots the Target a foote thorow, or better: which was strange, being that a Pistoll could not pierce it. Wee seeing the force of his Bowe, afterwards set him up a steele Target; he shot again, and burst his arrow all to pieces, he presently pulled out another Arrow, and bit it in his teeth, and seemed to bee in a great rage, so hee went away in great anger. Their Bowes are made of tough Hasell,[46] their strings of Leather, their Arrowes of Canes or Hasell, headed with very sharpe stones, and are made artificially like a broad Arrow: other some of their Arrowes are headed with the ends of Deeres hornes, and are feathered very artificially. Pasphia was as good as his word; for hee sent Venison, but the Sawse[47] came within few dayes after.

At Port Cotage in our Voyage up the River, we saw a Savage Boy about the age of ten yeeres, which had a head of haire of a perfect yellow and a reasonable white skinne, which is a Miracle amongst all Savages.[48]

This River which wee have discovered is one of the famousest Rivers that ever was found by any Christian, it ebbes and flowes a hundred and threescore miles where ships of great burthen may harbour in safetie. Wheresoever we landed upon this River, wee saw the goodliest Woods as Beech, Oke, Cedar, Cypresse, Wal-nuts, Sassafras and Vines in great abundance, which hang in great clusters on many Trees, and other Trees unknowne, and all the grounds bespred with many sweet and delicate

---

[44] A small shield.
[45] An English ell was forty-five inches long.
[46] Hazel.
[47] Presumably sauce.
[48] The "Savage Boy" was possibly a child of survivors of Roanoke; not until the end of 1608, after Percy had written his account, did settlers in Jamestown know that the Roanoke colonists were dead. See Kupperman, *Roanoke,* 137.

flowres of divers colours and kindes. There are also many fruites as Strawberries, Mulberries, Rasberries and Fruits unknowne, there are many branches of this River, which runne flowing through the Woods with great plentie of fish of all kindes, as for Sturgeon all the World cannot be compared to it. In this Countrey I have seene many great and large Medowes having excellent good pasture for any Cattle. There is also great store of Deere both Red and Fallow. There are Beares, Foxes, Otters, Bevers, Muskats, and wild beasts unknowne.

The foure and twentieth day wee set up a Crosse at the head of this River, naming it Kings River, where we proclaimed James King of England to have the most right unto it. When wee had finished and set up our Crosse, we shipt our men and made for James Fort. By the way[49] wee came to Pohatans Towre where the Captaine went on shore suffering none to goe with him, hee presented the Commander of this place with a Hatchet which hee tooke joyfully, and was well pleased.

But yet the Savages murmured at our planting in the Countrie, whereupon this Werowance made answere againe very wisely of a Savage, Why should you bee offended with them as long as they hurt you not, nor take any thing away by force, they take but a litle waste ground, which doth you nor any of us any good.

I saw Bread made by their women which doe all their drugerie.[50] The men takes their pleasure in hunting and their warres, which they are in continually one Kingdome against another. The manner of baking of bread is thus, after they pound their wheat into flowre with hote water, they make it into paste, and worke it into round balls and Cakes, then they put it into a pot of seething water, when it is sod throughly, they lay it on a smooth stone, there they harden it as well as in an Oven.

There is notice to be taken to know married women from Maids, the Maids you shall alwayes see the fore part of their head and sides shaven close, the hinder part very long, which they tie in a pleate hanging downe to their hips. The married women weares their haire all of a length, and is tied of that fashion that the Maids are. The women kinde in this Countrey doth pounce and race[51] their bodies, legges, thighes, armes and faces with a sharpe Iron, which makes a stampe in curious knots, and drawes the proportion of Fowles, Fish, or Beasts, then with paintings of sundry lively colours, they rub it into the stampe which will never be taken away, because it is dried into the flesh where it is sered.

---

[49] Along the way.
[50] Drudgery.
[51] Prick and cut the skin in a design; tattoo.

The Savages beare their yeeres well, for when wee were at Pamon-kies,[52] wee saw a Savage by their report was above eight score[53] yeeres of age. His eyes were sunke into his head, having never a tooth in his mouth, his haire all gray with a reasonable bigge beard, which was as white as any snow. It is a Miracle to see a Savage have any haire on their faces, I never saw, read, nor heard, any have the like before. This Savage was as lustie and went as fast as any of us, which was strange to behold.

The fifteenth day of June, we had built and finished our Fort which was triangle wise, having three Bulwarkes at every corner like a halfe Moone, and foure or five pieces of Artillerie mounted in them we had made our selves sufficiently strong for these Savages, we had also sowne most of our Corne on two Mountaines, it sprang a mans height from the ground, this Countrey is a fruitfull soile, bearing many goodly and fruitfull Trees, as Mulberries, Cherries, Walnuts, Ceders, Cypresse, Sassafras, and Vines in great abundance.

Munday the two and twentieth of June, in the morning Captaine Newport in the Admirall departed from James Port for England.

Captaine Newport being gone for England, leaving us (one hundred and foure persons) verie bare and scantie of victualls, furthermore in wares and in danger of the Savages. We hoped after a supply which Captaine Newport promised within twentie weekes. But if the beginners of this action doe carefully further us, the Country being so fruitfull, it would be as great a profit to the Realme of England, as the Indies to the King of Spaine, if this River which wee have found had beene discovered in the time of warre with Spaine, it would have been a commoditie to our Realme, and a great annoyance to our enemies. The seven and twentieth of July the King of Rapahanna, demanded a Canoa which was restored, lifted up his hand to the Sunne, which they worship as their God, besides he laid his hand on his heart, that he would be our speciall friend. It is a generall rule of these people when they swere by their God which is the Sunne, no Christian will keepe their Oath better upon this promise. These people have a great reverence to the Sunne above all other things at the rising and setting of the same, they sit downe lifting up their hands and eyes to the Sunne making a round Circle on the ground with dried Tobacco, then they began to pray making many Devillish gestures with a Hellish noise foming at the mouth, staring with their eyes, wagging their heads and hands in such a fashion and deformitie as it was monstrous to behold.

---

[52] Pamunkey is a river in eastern Virginia.
[53] One hundred sixty years.

The sixt of August there died John Asbie of the bloudie Fluxe.[54] The ninth day died George Flowre of the swelling.[55] The tenth day died William Bruster Gentleman, of a wound given by the Savages, and was buried the eleventh day.

The fourteenth day, Jerome Alikock Ancient, died of a wound, the same day Francis Midwinter, Edward Moris Corporall died suddenly.

The fifteenth day, there died Edward Browne and Stephen Galthrope. The sixteenth day, there died Thomas Gower Gentleman. The seventeenth day, there died Thomas Mounslic. The eighteenth day, there died Robert Pennington, and John Martine Gentleman. The nineteenth day, died Drue Piggase Gentleman. The two and twentieth day of August, there died Captaine Bartholomew Gosnold one of our Councell, he was honourably buried, having all the Ordnance in the Fort shot off with many vollies of small shot.

After Captaine Gosnols death, the Councell could hardly agree by the dissention of Captaine Kendall, which afterward was committed about hainous matters which was proved against him.

The foure and twentieth day, died Edward Harington and George Walker, and were buried the same day. The sixe and twentieth day, died Kenelme Throgmortine. The seven and twentieth day died William Roods. The eight and twentieth day died Thomas Stoodie, Cape Merchant.

The fourth day of September died Thomas Jacob Sergeant. The fift day, there died Benjamin Beast. Our men were destroyed with cruell diseases as Swellings, Fluxes, Burning Fevers, and by warres, and some departed suddenly, but for the most part they died of meere famine. There were never Englishmen left in a forreigne Countrey in such miserie as wee were in this new discovered Virginia. Wee watched every three nights lying on the bare cold ground what weather soever came warded all the next day, which brought our men to bee most feeble wretches, our food was but a small Can of Barlie sod in water to five men a day, our drinke cold water taken out of the River, which was at a floud verie salt, at a low tide full of slime and filth, which was the destruction of many of our men. Thus we lived for the space of five moneths in this miserable distresse, not having five able men to man our Bulwarkes upon any occasion. If it had not pleased God to have put a terrour in the Savages hearts, we had all

---

[54] Dysentery.

[55] Probably due to dysentery, though possibly caused by salt intoxication from salt that invaded river water. See Carville Earle, "Environment, Disease, and Mortality in Early Virginia," in Thad W. Tate and David L. Ammerman, eds., *The Chesapeake in the Seventeenth Century: Essays on Anglo-American Society and Politics* (Chapel Hill: University of North Carolina Press, 1979), 96–125.

perished by those vild and cruell Pagans, being in that weake estate as we were; our men night and day groaning in every corner of the Fort most pittifull to heare, if there were any conscience in men, it would make their harts to bleed to heare the pittiful murmurings & out-cries of our sick men without reliefe every night and day for the space of sixe weekes, some departing out of the World, many times three or foure in a night, in the morning their bodies trailed out of their Cabines like Dogges to be buried: in this sort did I see the mortalitie of divers of our people.

It pleased God, after a while, to send those people which were our mortall enemies to releeve us with victuals, as Bread, Corne, Fish, and Flesh in great plentie, which was the setting up of our feeble men, otherwise wee had all perished. Also we were frequented by divers Kings in the Countrie, bringing us store of provision to our great comfort.

The eleventh day, there was certaine Articles laid against Master Wingfield which was then President, thereupon he was not only displaced out of his President ship, but also from being of the Councell. Afterwards Captaine John Ratcliffe was chosen President.

The eighteenth day, died one Ellis Kinistone which was starved to death with cold. The same day at night, died one Richard Simmons. The nineteenth day, there died one Thomas Mouton.

William White (having lived with the Natives) reported to us of their customes in the morning by breake of day, before they eate or drinke both men, women and children, that be above tenne yeeres of age runnes into the water, there washes themselves a good while till the Sunne riseth, then offer Sacrifice to it, strewing Tobacco on the water or Land, honouring the Sunne as their God, likewise they doe at the setting of the Sunne.

7

ANONYMOUS

A True Declaration of the Estate of the Colonie in Virginia
(Issued by the Virginia Company)
1610

Early reports from Jamestown revealed that diseases in the Chesapeake Bay region could bring death to any English migrant who traveled there. These reports, or perhaps the rumors they engendered among potential travelers who had gathered in London and at other British ports seeking employment, could have had a disastrous impact on the Virginia Company. The organizers of the company knew that its survival depended on recruiting would-be settlers, and they believed that many would be dissuaded by accounts of disease and death in the nascent colony. The company's directors must have understood the lesson of the Roanoke experience all too well: Any colony that did not receive sufficient people and support from England could disappear, along with whatever resources investors had sunk into the project.

To counter the doomsaying reports, the company circulated an anonymous pamphlet, the full title of which read A True Declaration of the Estate of the Colonie in Virginia, with a Confutation of Such Scandalous Reports as Have Tended to the Disgrace of So Worthy an Enterprise. *As the historian David B. Quinn has aptly noted, it is perhaps "the most distinguished piece of propaganda for the colony and its best apologia." It is difficult to imagine a place that needed more sorely than Virginia some propaganda to support it and an apologia for what was going on there.*

The report itself contained both a justification for the establishment of colonies in general and information intended to combat any negative images of Virginia then being circulated. Like other propaganda pamphlets, the anonymous author cited ancient writers as justification for the establishment of colonies and followed with a brief summary of English colonists who had traveled to Virginia by way of Bermuda, an "inchaunted pile of rockes, and a desert inhabitation for Divels." Part of the tract treated the calamities that

---

A True Declaration of the Estate of the Colonie in Virginia, in David Beers Quinn and Alison O. Quinn, eds. *New American World,* 5 vols. (New York and London: Macmillan, 1979), 5:248–62.

had befallen the first colonists, including the murder of a woman colonist by her husband, who claimed that after killing her "he hid her to satisfie his hunger, and that he fed daily upon her." But such travails could be overcome, the pamphlet author believed, and in the section reprinted here he detailed the many benefits (particularly economic) to be derived from continued colonization in Jamestown. By traveling to America future migrants would be taking the path to their own material success and the prosperity of the nation. They would not have to do so alone. The company reorganized itself in 1609 and recruited able men to lead the effort. Thomas West (1577–1618), Baron De La Warre, accepted the governorship of Virginia and arrived in Jamestown in June 1610. Upon his arrival he encountered Sir Thomas Gates (d. 1621), whose expedition to Virginia had been waylaid in Bermuda. Gates had brought provisions with him that the Jamestown settlers sorely needed and later received credit from John Smith for keeping many of the settlers alive during a time of acute hardship. The colonists continued to suffer during this period from diseases and near-starvation, and the Virginia Company hoped that the change in command would improve conditions in Jamestown.

Who do you think was the intended audience for this pamphlet—potential migrants or English officials who were perhaps becoming wary of overseas investments? What were the author's main appeals for continued colonization of Jamestown? Which of the arguments would have been most persuasive to a potential migrant? Is the tone of this pamphlet closer to that of the Hakluyts and Peckham or of Percy? Did it matter that the pamphlet, unlike many other promotional accounts, was written anonymously?

The fertility of the soile, the temperature of the climate, the form of government, the condition of our people, their daily invocating of the name of God, being thus expressed; Why should the successe (by the rules of mortall judgement) be despaired? Why should not the rich harvest of our hopes be seasonably expected? I dare say, that the resolution of Caesar in Fraunce, the designes of Alexander in Greece, the discoveries of Hernando Cortes in the West, and of Emanuel, King of Portugale in the East, were not incouraged upon so firme grounds of state and possibility. All which I could demonstrate out of their owne Records, were I not prevented with hast, to satisfie their longings, who with an open eare, hearken after the commodities of the countrey: whose appetites I will no longer frustrate, then their eyes can runne over this succinct Narration.

I called it a succinct Narration, because the commodities in former

Treatises have beene largely described, which I will here only epitomise,[1] lest any man should change his resolution, when the same grounds remaine, which were the cause of his former adventure.

The Councell of Virginia (finding the smalnesse of that returne, which they hoped should have defraied the charge of a new supply) entred into a deepe consultation, and propounded amongst themselves, whether it were fit to enter into a new contribution, or in time to send for home the Lord La-ware, and to abandon the action. They resolved to send for sir Thomas Gates, who being come, they adjured[2] him to deale plainely with them, and to make a true relation of those things which were presently to be had, or hereafter to be hoped for in Virginia. Sir Thomas Gates with a solemne and sacred oath replied, that all things before reported were true: that the country yeeldeth abundance of wood, as Oake, Wainscot,[3] Walnut trees, Bay trees, Ashe, Sarsafrase, live Oake, greene all the yeare, Cedar and Firre; which are the materials, of soape ashes, and pot ashes,[4] of oyles of walnuts, and bayes, of pitch[5] and tarre, of Clap boards, Pipestaves, Masts and excellent boardes of forty, fifty and sixtie length, and three foote bredth, when one Firre tree is able to make the maine Mast of the greatest ship in England. He avouched, that there are incredible variety of sweet woods, especially of the Balsamum tree, which distilleth a pretious gum; that there are innumerable White Mulberry trees, which in so warme a climate may cherish and feede millions of silke wormes, and returne us in a very short time, as great a plenty of silke as is vented[6] into the whole world from al the parts of Italy: that there are divers sorts of Minerals, especially of Iron oare, lying upon the ground for ten miles circuite; (of which we have made triall at home, that it maketh as good Iron as any is in Europe:) that a kinde of hempe or flax, and silke grasse doe grow there naturally, which will affoord stuffe for all manner of excellent Cordage:[7] that the river swarmeth with Sturgeon; the land aboundeth with Vines, the woodes doe harbor exceeding store of Beavers, Foxes and Squirrils, the waters doe nourish a great encrease of Otters; all which are covered with pretious furres: that there are in present discovered dyes and drugs of sundry qualities; that the Orenges which have beene planted did prosper in the winter, which is an infallible argument, that Lym-

---

[1]Summarize.
[2]Commanded him as if under oath.
[3]A superior quality of oak, suitable for use as paneling.
[4]The ash from certain trees was used to make lye for soap; potassium carbonate (potash), also derived from wood ashes, was used for fertilizer (among other things).
[5]A dark, resinous substance used to protect wood from moisture.
[6]Marketed.
[7]Rope.

mons, sugar Canes, Almonds, Rice, Anniseede, and all other commodities which we have from the Staights,[8] may be supplied to us in our owne countrey, and by our owne industry: that the corne yeeldeth a trebble encrease more then ours; and lastly, that it is one of the goodliest countries under the sunne; enterveined with five maine Rivers, and promising as rich entrals[9] as any Kingdome of the earth, to whom the sunne is so neerer a neighbour.

What these things will yeelde, the Merchant best knoweth, who findeth by experience, that many hundreth of thousands of pounds are yearly spent in Christendome in these commodities. The Merchant knoweth, that Caveare and Traine[10] which come from Russia, can be brought hither but once in the yeare, in regard of the Ice: and that Sturgeon which is brought from the East countries, can come but twice a yeare; and that not before the end of Aprill, or the beginning of May; which many times in regard of the heat of those moneths, is tainted in the transportation: when from Virginia they may be brought to us in foure and twenty daies, and in al the colde seasons of the yeare. The Merchants know, that the commodity of sope and pot ashes are very scant in Prussia; that they are brought three hundred miles by land, and three hundred miles by rivers, before they come to the Sea; that they pay a custome there, and another in Denmarke, which enhanceth the prices exceedingly: But in Virginia they may have them without carriage by land or custome (because five Navigable Rivers doe lead up five several waies into the bowels of the whole countrey.) As therefore the like Rivers, are the cause of the riches of Holland, so will these be to us a wondrous cause of saving of expences. The merchant knoweth, that through the troubles in Poland & Muscovy,[11] (whose eternall warres are like the Antipathy of the Dragon & Elephants) all their traffique[12] for Mastes, Deales, Pitch, Tarre, Flax, Hempe, and Cordage, are every day more and more indangered, and the woods of those countries are almost exhausted. All which are to be had in Virginia with farre lesse charge, and farre more safety. Lastly, the Merchant knoweth, that for our commodities in the Staights, as sweet wines, orenges, lemmonds, anniseeds, &c. that we stand at the devotion of politique Princes and States, who for their proper utility, devise all courses to grinde our merchants, all pretences to confiscate their goods, and to draw from us al marrow of gaine by their inquisitive inventions: when in

[8]Straits of Gibraltar, through which the Mediterranean trade passed.
[9]Entry.
[10]Caviar and train oil, the latter obtained from the blubber of seals and whales.
[11]Russian principality centered around Moscow.
[12]Trade, commerce.

Virginia, a few yeares labour by planting and husbandry, will furnish all our defects, with honour and security; especially since the Frenchmen (who are with the Lord Governour)[13] do confidently promise, that within two yeares we may expect a plentifull Vintage.

When therefore this noble enterprise, by the rules of Religion is expressly justified; when the passages by Sea are all open and discovered; when the climate is so fruitfully tempered; when the naturall riches of the soile are so powerfully confirmed: will any man so much betray his owne inconsiderate ignorance, and bewray[14] his rashnesse; that when the same Sunne shineth, he should not have the same eies to beholde it; when the same hope remaines, he should not have the same heart to apprehend it? At the voyage of Sir Thomas Gates, what swarmes of people desired to be transported? what alacrity and cheerefulnesse in the Adventurers by free wil offerings, to build up this new Tabernacle?[15] Shall we now be dejected? Shall we cast downe our heads like Bull rushes? because one storme at sea hath deferred our joyes and comforts! We are too effeminate in our longings, and too impatient of delaies. Gods al-disposing providence, is not compellable by mans violence: Let any wisedome give a solide reason, why his purpose should be changed, when those grounds which gave life to his first purpose, are not changed. It is but a golden slumber, that dreameth of any humane felicity, which is not sauced with some contingent miserie. Dolor & voluptas, invicem cedunt,[16] Greife and pleasure are the crosse sailes of the worlds ever-turning-windmill. Let no man therefore be over wise, to cast beyond the moone and to multiplie needlesse doubts and questions. . . .

To wade a little further, who ever saluted the monuments of antiquity, and doth not finde, that Carthage aspired to be Empresse of the world, by her opportunity of havens and multitude of shipping? What hindereth the great Mahumetane[17] Prince, from seazing upon al the territories of Europe, but onely the want of skilfull marriners? What created the rich and free states of Holland, but their winged Navy? It was a fit embleme that painted death standing upon the shoares of Fraunce, Germany and Spaine, and looking over into England: intymating unto us, that so long as we are Lords of the narrow seas, death stands on the other shoares, and onely can looke upon us: but if our wooden wals were ruinated, death would soone make a bridge to come over, and devoure our Nation. When

[13]La Warre.
[14]Expose.
[15]Dwelling.
[16]"Grief and pleasure in turn are present."
[17]The sultan of the Ottoman Empire, defeated in the Mediterranean at the Battle of Lepanto in 1571.

therefore our mils of Iron, and excesse of building, have already turned our greatest woods into pasture and champion,[18] within these few years; neither the scattered Forrests of England, nor the diminished Groves of Ireland, will supply the defect of our Navy. When in Virginia there is nothing wanting, but onely mens labours, to furnish both Prince, State and merchant, without charge or difficulty. Againe, whither shall wee transport our cloth, and how shall we sustaine our Artisans? Shall we send it into Turkey? Some private and deceitfull avarice hath discredited our merchandize. Into Spaine? it aboundeth with sheepe and wooll. Into Poland and Muscovy? the daunger doth overballance the gaine in times of contention. Into Fraunce and Germany? they are for the most part supplied by their owne peace. When if our Colony were peopled in Virginia, mutabit vellera merces,[19] we shall exchange our store of cloth for other merchandize. Let any man resolve why the Councell of Virginia, doe now most earnestly continue their adventures? why those that were (eye witnesses) of the former supposed miseries, do voluntarily returne with joy and comfort? why those noble and worthy personages, doe offer to make the action good upon the hazard of their lives & fortunes? And why Sir Thomas Gates longeth and hasteneth to go thither again, and the Lord La-ware desireth so earnestly to stay there? Are not all these things as deere to them as to any other of the Adventurers? Have not their hopes the same wings? their feares the same fetters? their estates the same rockes? their lives and soules greater gulfes of perill and despair? And yet neither the imbracements of their wives, nor indulgence to their babes, nor the neglect of their domesticke fortunes, nor banishment from their native soile, nor any experimented dangers have broken their noble resolution.

---

[18]An expanse of level, open country.
[19]"Cloth will be turned into other goods."

8

JOHN WINTHROP

"Reasons to Be Considered for Justifying the Undertakers of the Intended Plantation in New England and for Encouraging Such Whose Hearts God Shall Move to Join with Them in It"

1629

English Puritans started to emigrate to New England in 1620 and soon founded Plymouth (in present-day Massachusetts) under the direction of William Bradford and others. During the 1620s, more Puritans crossed the Atlantic. The largest exodus, involving perhaps as many as twenty-one thousand English men and women, took place from 1630 to 1642. The event is often referred to as the "Great Migration" even though it was briefer and involved fewer people than the seventeenth-century migration to the English colonies on the shores of Chesapeake Bay. The Great Migration was led by, among others, John Winthrop, who became the first governor of the Massachusetts Bay colony, which was established in 1629.

Like other promoters of colonization, Winthrop (1588–1649) had been highly educated (at Cambridge University) and was a lawyer. Unlike those who promoted settlements along the Chesapeake, Winthrop was a Puritan, one of a group of Protestants who fled England to avoid persecution for their religious beliefs. Many Puritans lived and worked in towns in England and, in the years preceding their migration, suffered periodic economic setbacks, particularly in the textile industry. The dual discomforts of religious persecution and economic recession convinced many Puritans to cross the Atlantic. In New England they hoped to create a "bible commonwealth," a society where religious observance would be vital to daily life.

As governor of the Massachusetts Bay Colony, Winthrop played a major role in the initial organization of the settlements there. He did so in part through his public statements. In 1630, en route to New England aboard the

John Winthrop, "Reasons to Be Considered for Justifying the Undertakers of the Intended Plantation in New England and for Encouraging Such Whose Hearts God Shall Move to Join with Them in It," Massachusetts Historical Society *Proceedings* 8 (1864–1865), 420–25.

ship Arbella, *he delivered "A Model of Christian Charity," one of the most famous sermons in American history. The Puritans, he declared, "must consider that we shall be as a city upon a hill." The image was compelling, for Winthrop urged that the city could become a model for the rest of the world, a beacon of light that could show others how to establish a godly community on earth. But Winthrop also recognized the potential for failure. He knew that if the Puritans dealt "falsely with our God in this work we have undertaken," then "[w]e shall open the mouths of enemies to speak evil of the ways of God, and all professors for God's sake."[1] The stakes in the colonization venture could not have been higher.*

The year before Winthrop delivered that sermon, he wrote his "Reasons to Be Considered" to justify the Puritans' plans. It reveals, more plainly than many other Puritan documents, the arguments used to convince any doubters of the righteousness of their scheme. Winthrop's audience for this tract was other Puritans, many of whom believed that migration across the ocean was an inappropriate way to confront the challenges facing them in England. To defend the migration, Winthrop summarized his views about the plight of Puritans, and religion in general, in England. He also justified the Puritans' seizure of Indian lands in New England.

How did Winthrop justify the Puritans' right to settle on Indian land? How did his "Reasons" differ from the justifications of Sir Walter Ralegh or the Virginia Company? What role did God play in Winthrop's scheme? What do his views on Indian lands reveal about the Puritans' approach to the native peoples of New England?

First, It wilbe a service to the Church of great consequence to carry the Gospell into those p[ts]. of the world, to help on the cominge in of fulnesse of the Gentiles and to rayse a Bulworke against the kingdome of Antichrist, w[ch]. the Jesuites labour to rear up in those parts.[2]

2. All other Churches of Europe are brought to desolation and o[r] sinnes for w[ch]. the lord beginns already to frowne uppon us, doe threaten us fearfully, & who knowes but that god hath provided this place to be a

---

[1] John Winthrop, "A Model of Christian Charity," in Alan Heimert and Andrew Delbanco, eds., *The Puritans in America: A Narrative Anthology* (Cambridge: Harvard University Press, 1985), 91.

[2] Jesuit missionaries, who accompanied French colonizers and who had been present in North America since 1604, had been trying, with some success, to convert American Indians to Catholicism. Since the Puritans despised the Catholic church and the religious tenets of most Catholics, they felt they needed to halt the influence of the Jesuits and to inculcate Protestant beliefs among the Indians.

refuge for many whom he meanes to save out of the generall callamitie, and seeinge the Church hath no place lefte to flie into but the wildernesse what better worke cann there be, then to goe before & provide Tabernacles,[3] and food for her, against she cometh thither.

3. This land growes weary of her Inhabitants, soe as man whoe is ye most pretious of all creatures is heer more vile & base then the Earth we Tread uppon, & of lesse price among us, then a horse or a sheep, masters are forced by authoritie to entertaine servants, parents to maintaine their owne children, All Townes complaine of the burthen of their poore though we have taken up many unnessessary, yea unlawfull trades to mainteaine them, And we use the authoritie of the law to hinder the increase of people as urging the execution of the State against Cottages & Inmates & thus it is come to passe that Children, servants & neighbo^rs (especially if the be poore) are counted the greatest burthen wch if things were right it would be the cheifest earthly blessinge.[4]

4. The whole earth is the lords Garden & he hath given it to the sonnes of men, wth a generall Condition, Gen:1.28. Increase & multiply, replenish the earth & subdue it, wch was againe renewed to Noah, the end is Double morall & naturall that man might injoy the fruites of the earth & god might have his due glory from the creature, why then should we stand hear striveing for places of habitation, (many men spending as much labo^r & cost to recover or keep somtymes a Acre or two of land as would procure them many hundred as good or better in an other country) and in ye mean tyme suffer a whole Continent, as fruitfull & convenient for the use of man to lie waste w^thout any improvement.

5. We are growne to that height of intemperance in all excesse of riot, as noe mans estate almost will suffice to keep saile wth his equalls, & he who failes herein must live in scorne & contempt, hence it comes that all arts & trades are carried in that deceiptfull & unrighteous course, as it is almost impossible for a good & upright man to maintaine his charge and live comfortably in any of them.

6. The fountaines of learning & religion are soe corrupted (as beside the unsupportable charge of the education) most Children (even the best witts & fairest hopes) are perverted corrupted and utterly overthrowen, by the multitude of evill examples and the licentious gov^rm^t of those

---

[3] Dwelling places.
[4] A "statute of 1589 prohibited the erection of any cottage on fewer than four acres of land, which was judged the minimum necessary for supporting a family. The harboring of 'inmates' became an increasing problem in the seventeenth century as casual, untaxed inhabitants threatened to become a burden on the poor rates." Heimert and Delbanco, *The Puritans in America*, 71n.

Seminaries, where men straine at Gnats, & swallow Camells,[5] use all severity for maintenance of cappes,[6] & other accomplements[7] but suffer all Ruffian-like fashion & disorder in manners to passe uncontrowled.

7. What cann be a better worke & more hono[rble] & worthy a Christian then to help rayse & support a particular church while it is in the infancy, & to Joyne his forces wth such a company of faithfull people as by a tymely assistance may growe stronge and prosper, and for want of it may be put to great hazard, if not wholely ruined.

8. If any such whoe are knowen to be godly, & live in wealth and prosperity here shall forsake all this to joyne themselves to this church & to runn a hazard wth them of a hard & meane condition it wilbe an example of great use both for removeing the scandall of wordly & sinister respects w[ch] is cast uppon the adventurers to give more life to the faith of Gods people in their prayers for the plantation & to encourage other to joyne the more willingly in it.

9. It appeares to be a worke of god, for the good of his church in that he hath disposed the harts of soe many of his wise & faithfull servants (both ministers & others) not only to approve of the enterprise but to interest themselves in it, som in their persons & estates, others by their serious advise & helpe otherwise: And all by their prayers for the welfare of it, Amos 3. The lord revealeth his Secretts to his servants the Prophets, it is likely he hath some great worke in hand w[ch] he hath revealed to his prophets among us, whom he hath stirred upp to encourage his servants to this plantation for he doth not use to seduce his people by his owne Prophets, but comitts that office to the ministery of false prophets and lyinge spirits.

Divers objections w[ch] have been made against this plantation wth their answeares and resolutions.

Ob: 1: We have noe warrant[8] to enter uppon that land w[ch] hath been soe long possessed by others.

Answ: 1: That w[ch] lies comon & hath never been replenished or subdued is free to any that will possesse and improve it, for god hath given to the sonnes of men a double right to the earth, there is a naturall right & a Civill right the first right was naturall when men held the earth in

---

[5] Reference to Matt. 23:24, i.e., they pay undue attention to minor matters and neglect the important ones.

[6] Perhaps a reference to a symbol of power or hierarchy, the "cap of maintenance" was a cap borne as one of the insignia of office before the sovereign of England at the coronation and before mayors of some cities.

[7] Adornments.

[8] Authorization.

common every man soweing, and feeding where he pleased: and then as men and the cattle increased they appropriated certaine parcells of ground by enclosing, and peculier manurance,[9] and this in tyme gave them a Civill right. . . . [Winthrop goes on to provide a lengthy biblical justification for the Puritans' right to the land. — ED.] And for the Natives in New England they inclose noe land neither have any setled habitation nor any tame cattle to improve the land by, & soe have noe other but a naturall right to those countries Soe as if wee leave them sufficient for their use wee may lawfully take the rest, there being more then enough for them & us.

2. We shall come in wth the good leave of the Natives, who finde benefitt already by our neighbourhood & learne of us to improve put to more use, then before they could doe the whole, & by this meanes wee come in by valuable purchase: for they hav of us that w[ch] will yeild them more benefitt then all the land w[ch] wee have from them.

3. God hath consumed the Natives wth a great plague in those parts soe as there be few in-habitants left.

Objec. 2. It wilbe a great wrong to our church to take awaie the good people & we shall lay it the more open to the judgment feared.

Answ: 1. The departinge of good people from a country doth not cause a judgment but foreshew it, w[ch] maie occasion such as remaine to turne from their evill waies that they may prevent it, or to take some other course that they may escape it.

2. Such as goe away are of noe observation in respects of those whoe remaine & they are likely to doe more good there then heer, & since Christ's tyme the church is to be considered as universall w[th]out distinction of countries, soe as he who doeth good in any once place, serves the church in all places in regard of the unitie.

3. It is the revealed will of god that the gospell should be preached to all nations, and though we know not whether those Barbarians will receive it at first or not, yett it is a good worke to serve gods providence in offering it to them, & this is fittest to be done by gods owne servants for god shall have glory by it, though they refuse it, & there is good hope that the posterity shall by this meanes be gathered into Christ's Sheepfold.

Ob: 3. We have feared a judgment a great while, but yett wee are safe it were better therefor to stay till it come, & either wee may flie then or if we be overtaken in it, we may well content our selves to suffer wth such a church as ours is.

Answ: It is likely this consideration made the churches beyond the seas, as, the Palatinate, Rochell &c.[10] to sitt still at home & not to looke

---

[9] Tenure, occupation.

[10] La Pallice and La Rochelle, two places in this age of religious wars where Catholics under Cardinal Richelieu had defeated the French Huguenots.

out for shelter while they might have found it, but the woefull spectacle of their ruine, may teach us more wisedome, to avoyd the plage when it is foreseen, & not to tarry as they did till it overtake us, if they were now at their former liberty, we might be sure they would take other courses for their saftie & though half of them had miscarried in their escape, yett hadd it not be soe miserable to themselves nor scandalous to religion as this desperate bakeslidinge, & abjuringe the truth, wch many of the Antient professo^{rs} among them, & the whole posteritie wch remaine, are now plaged into.

Ob: 4. The ill successe of other plantations may tell us what wilbecome of this.

Answ: 1. None of the former susteyned any great damage, but Virginia which happened through their owne sloth & securitie.[11]

2. The argum^t is not good, for thus it stands, some plantations have miscarried therefore we should not make any, it consists in particulars & soe concludes nothinge, we might as well reason thus, many houses have been burnt by Kilnes,[12] therefore we should use none, many shipps have been cast away, therefore we should content our selves wth our home commodities, & not adventure mens lives at Sea for those things wch wee might live wthout, some men have been undone by being advanced to great places therefore we should refuse our p^{r}ferment,[13] &c.

3. The fruite of any publicke designe is not to be discerned by the imediate successe, it may appear in tyme that former plantations were all to good use.

4. There were great and fundamentall errors in the former wch are like to be avoyded in this, for first their maine end was Carnall & not Religious, secondly they used unfitt instruments a multitude of rude & misgov^{r}ned persons, the very scumme of the people, thirdly they did not establish a right forme of government.

Ob: 5. It is attended[14] wth many & great difficulties.

Answ: Soe is every good action, the heathen could say Ardua virtutis via.[15] And they way of gods kingdome (The best way in the world) is accompanied wth most difficulties, Straight is the gate & narrow is the way that leadeth to life, againe the difficulties are noe other then such as many dayly meet wth and such as god hath brought others well through them.

Ob: 6. It is a work above the power of the undertakers.

Answ: 1. The welfare of any body consists not soe much in quantity as

---

[11] Laziness and complacence; Winthrop blames the colonists themselves for the troubles sustained in early Virginia (see Document 6).

[12] Ovens.

[13] Preferment; i.e., betterment, advancement.

[14] Accompanied.

[15] "The difficult path of virtue."

in due proportion & disposition of par^tes & wee see other plantations have subsisted divers years & prospered from weake meanes.

2. It is noe wonder for great things may arise from weake contemptable beginnings, it hath been oft seen in kingedomes & states & may as well hold in towns & plantations. The Waldenses[16] were scartered into the Alpes & mountaines of Piedmont, by small companies, but they became famous churches whereof some remaine to this day & it is certaine that the Turkes, Venetians & other states were very weake in there beginninge.

Ob: 7. The country affords noe naturall fortifications.

Answ: Noe more did Holland & many other places wch had greater enemies & nearer at hand & God doth use to place his people in the middest of perills that they may trust in him and not in outward means & saftie, soe when he would chuse a place to plant his beloved people in he seateth them not in an Ileland or other place fortified by nature, but in a plaine country besett wth potent and bitter enemies round about, yett soe long as they served him & trusted in his help they were safe. Soe the Apostle Paule saith of him self & his fellow labourers that they were compassed[17] wth dangers one every side, & were daily under the sentence of death that they might learne to trust in the liveinge God.

Ob: 8. The place affordeth noe comfortable meanes to the first planto^rs & our breedinge heer at home have made us unfitt for the hardshipp we are like to indure.

Answ: 1. Noe place of it self hath afforded sufficient to the first inhabitants, such things as we stand in need of are usually supplied by gods blessing uppon the wisedome & industrie of man & what soever wee stand in need of is treasured in the earth, by the Creato^r & is to be fetched thence by the sweat of o^r Browes.

2. Wee must learne wth Paule to want, as well as to abound, if we have food & raiment[18] (wch are there to be had) we ought to be contented, the difference in the quallity may a litle displease us but it cannot hurt us.

3. It may be by this meanes God will bringe us to repent of our former intemperance, & soe cure us of that disease, wch sends many amongst us untimelie to their graves and others to hell, soe he carried the Israelits into the wildernesse & made them forgett the flesh potts of Egypt, wch was sorie pinch[19] to them att first but he disposed to their good in th'end. Deutron. 30. 3. 16.

---

[16] The Waldensians were a group of radical Catholics, originating in the twelfth century, who believed that lay people should be able to read and interpret scripture; they also preached against corrupt clergy.

[17] Surrounded.

[18] Clothing.

[19] A hardship.

9

JOHN SMITH

A Description of New England
1616 and

Advertisements for the Unexperienced Planters
of New England, or Any Where
1631

Captain John Smith (1580–1631) was perhaps the most famous colonist during the first active phase of English colonization in North America. His fame spread from his dual career: as a leader of the settlement at Jamestown and as a promoter of colonization. No other contemporary English migrant left such a body of work behind, and few were able to match Smith's keen observations. His views on early America, not only developments along the Chesapeake but in New England as well, survive in a series of works, including A Description of New England *(London, 1616).* Advertisements for the Unexperienced Planters of New England, or Any Where, or, The Path-way to Experience to Erect a Plantation *(London, 1631), his last work, was published in the year of his death. This account brought together his most important ideas and became perhaps his most effective promotional effort.*

To Smith, the colonization of North America had enormous importance, and not only for the migrants who crossed the Atlantic or the Indians who would, according to virtually every English promotional plan, become good Protestants. For him, colonization was critical to England's future. Smith cringed at the criminal behavior of some English colonists because, as historian Nicholas Canny has noted, he thought that such miscreants threatened the greater moral purpose of overseas settlements: Colonization was "a means of saving England itself from succumbing to the degeneration that had beset all great societies in the past." How could such a noble pursuit survive if, as had already occurred, some colonists engaged in bestiality or

---

John Smith, *A Description of New England* and *Advertisements for the Unexperienced Planters of New England, or Any Where,* in Karen Ordahl Kupperman, ed. *Captain John Smith: A Select Edition of His Writings* (Chapel Hill: University of North Carolina Press, 1988), 241–49, 284–86.

sodomized young boys? The criminals who committed such acts, Smith believed, needed to be elminated if America was to help the English overcome their own problems at home.

In the excerpt included here from his Description of New England, *Smith echoed the ideas of earlier promoters, notably the two Richard Hakluyts. Smith described the religious motivation for colonies while recognizing the value of overseas settlements for English men and women unable to find jobs at home. Finally, he informed his readers of the strategic importance of colonies and reminded them that the English had missed a golden opportunity when Henry VII, following the wishes of his advisers, had turned down the overtures of Bartholomew Columbus (Christopher's brother) in 1489 to sail to Asia by heading west across the Atlantic. Had the English accepted that offer, the history of Europe would have been fundamentally changed. In the* Description, *Smith uses the earlier English failures in the sixteenth century to make his case for seizing opportunities that were then available.*

In the Advertisements, *Smith aimed to provide the information necessary for furthering English colonization efforts. He did not then need to convince a possibly skeptical audience of the need for colonies since Jamestown, in spite of the horrors experienced by settlers there, had already existed for almost a generation, and New England was beginning to attract larger numbers of Puritans than it had since its start in 1620. In the excerpt printed here, Smith rendered his final judgment on the need for colonies, and he did so in a more coherent way than in his earlier writing.*

In Smith's writings we grasp what colonization meant to one of the genuine leaders of the English settlement of North America. How did Smith's status influence his views? How do his views differ from those of earlier promoters? In what ways, if any, do these excerpts reveal that his views changed over time? What role did the history of European expansion efforts play in Smith's understanding of the English colonization of North America?

A DESCRIPTION OF NEW ENGLAND

Who can desire more content, that hath small meanes; or but only his merit to advance his fortune, then to tread, and plant that ground hee hath purchased by the hazard of his life? If he have but the taste of virtue, and magnanimitie,[1] what to such a minde can bee more pleasant, then planting and building a foundation for his Posteritie, gotte from the rude earth, by Gods blessing and his owne industrie, without prejudice to any? If hee

---

[1] Noble spirit.

have any graine of faith or zeale in Religion, what can hee doe lesse hurtfull
to any; or more agreeable to God, then to seeke to convert those poore
Salvages[2] to know Christ, and humanitie, whose labors with discretion will
triple requite thy charge and paines? What so truely sutes with honour and
honestie, as the discovering things unknowne? erecting Townes, peopling
Countries, informing the ignorant, reforming things unjust, teaching virtue; and gaine to our Native mother-countrie a kingdom to attend her;
finde imployment for those that are idle, because they know not what to
doe: so farre from wronging any, as to cause Posteritie to remember thee;
and remembring thee, ever honour that remembrance with praise? Consider: What were the beginnings and endings of the Monarkies of the
Chaldeans,[3] the Syrians, the Grecians,[4] and Romanes, but this one rule;
What was it they would not doe, for the good of the commonwealth, or
their Mother-citie? For example: Rome, What made her such a Monar-
chesse, but onely the adventures of her youth, not in riots at home; but in
dangers abroad? and the justice and judgement out of their experience,
when they grewe aged. What was their ruine and hurt, but this; The
excesse of idlenesse, the fondnesse[5] of Parents, the want of experience in
Magistrates, the admiration of their undeserved honours, the contempt of
true merit, their unjust jealosies, their politicke incredulities, their hypo-
criticall seeming goodnesse, and their deeds of secret lewdnesse? finally,
in fine, growing onely formall temporists,[6] all that their predecessors got
in many years, they lost in few daies. Those by their pains and vertues
became Lords of the world; they by their ease and vices became slaves to
their servants. This is the difference betwixt the use of Armes in the field,
and on the monuments of stones; the golden age and the leaden age,
prosperity and miserie, justice and corruption, substance and shadowes,
words and deeds, experience and imagination, making Commonwealths
and marring Commonwealths, the fruits of vertue and the conclusions of
vice.

Then, who would live at home idly (or thinke in himselfe any worth to
live) onely to eate, drink, and sleepe, and so die? Or by consuming that
carelesly, his friends got worthily? Or by using that miserably, that
maintained vertue honestly? Or, for being descended nobly, pine with the
vaine vaunt of great kindred, in penurie? Or (to maintaine a silly shewe of

---

[2] Savages; i.e., Indians.
[3] The Chaldeans were an ancient Semitic people in Babylonia.
[4] The Greeks.
[5] Foolish affection, unreasoning tenderness.
[6] A temporizer or procrastinator.

bravery) toyle out thy heart, soule, and time, basely, by shifts,[7] tricks, cards, and dice? Or by relating newes of others actions, sharke[8] here or there for a dinner, or supper; deceive thy friends, by faire promises, and dissimulation, in borrowing where thou never intendest to pay; offend the lawes, surfeit with excesse, burden thy Country, abuse thy selfe, despaire in want, and then couzen[9] thy kindred, yea even thine owne brother, and wish thy parents death (I will not say damnation) to have their estates? though thou seest what honours, and rewards, the world yet hath for them will seeke them and worthily deserve them.

I would be sory to offend, or that any should mistake my honest meaning: for I wish good to all, hurt to none. But rich men for the most part are growne to that dotage, through their pride in their wealth, as though there were no accident could end it, or their life. And what hellish care do such take to make it their owne miserie, and their Countries spoile, especially when there is most neede of their imployment? drawing by all manner of inventions, from the Prince and his honest subjects, even the vitall spirits of their powers and estates: as if their Bagges,[10] or Bragges, were so powerfull a defence, the malicious could not assault them; when they are the onely baite, to cause us not to be onely assaulted; but betrayed and murdered in our owne security, ere we well perceive it. . . .

My purpose is not to perswade children from their parents; men from their wives; nor servants from their masters: onely, such as with free consent may be spared: But that each parish, or village, in Citie, or Countrey, that will but apparell their fatherlesse children, of thirteene or fourteene years of age, or young maried people, that have small wealth to live on; heere by their labour may live exceeding well: provided alwaies that first there bee a sufficient power to command them, houses to receive them, meanes to defend them, and meet provisions for them; for, any place may bee overlain:[11] and it is most necessarie to have a fortresse (ere this grow to practice) and sufficient masters (as, Carpenters, Masons, Fishers, Fowlers, Gardiners, Husbandmen, Sawyers, Smiths, Spinsters, Taylors, Weavers, and such like) to take ten, twelve, or twentie, or as ther is occasion, for Apprentises. The Masters by this may quicklie growe rich; these may learne their trades themselves, to doe the like; to a

[7] Expedient or forced measures.
[8] To sponge on or swindle, to live like a parasite.
[9] Deceive.
[10] Money bags; i.e., wealth.
[11] Suffocated, overpopulated.

generall and an incredible benefit, for King, and Countrey, Master, and Servant.

It would bee an historie of a large volume, to recite the adventures of the Spanyards, and Portugals, their affronts, and defeats, their dangers and miseries; which with such incomparable honour and constant resolution, so farre beyond beleefe, they have attempted and indured in their discoveries and plantations, as may well condemne us, of too much imbecillitie, sloth, and negligence: yet the Authors of those new inventions, were held as ridiculous, for a long time, as now are others, that doe but seek to imitate their unparalleled vertues. And though we see daily their mountaines of wealth (sprong from the plants of their generous indevours) yet is our sensualitie and untowardnesse[12] such, and so great, that wee either ignorantly beleeve nothing; or so curiously[13] contest, to prevent wee knowe not what future events; that wee either so neglect, or oppresse and discourage the present, as wee spoile all in the making, crop all in the blooming; and building upon faire sand, rather then rough rockes, judge that wee knowe not, governe that wee have not, feare that which is not; and for feare some should doe too well, force such against their willes to be idle or as ill. And who is he hath judgement, courage, and any industrie or qualitie with understanding, will leave his Countrie, his hopes at home, his certaine estate, his friends, pleasures, libertie, and the preferment sweete England doth afford to all degrees, were it not to advance his fortunes by injoying his deserts? whose prosperitie once appearing, will incourage others: but it must be cherished as a childe, till it be able to goe, and understand it selfe; and not corrected, nor oppressed above its strength, ere it knowe wherefore. A child can neither performe the office,[14] nor deedes of a man of strength, nor indure that affliction He is able; nor can an Apprentice at the first performe the part of a Maister. And if twentie yeeres bee required to make a child a man, seven yeares limited an apprentice for his trade: if scarce an age be sufficient to make a wise man a States man; and commonly, a man dies ere he hath learned to be discreet: If perfection be so hard to be obtained, as of necessitie there must bee practice, as well as theorick: Let no man much condemne this paradox opinion, to say, that halfe seven yeeres is scarce sufficient, for a good capacitie, to learne in these affaires, how to carrie himselfe: and who ever shall trie in these remote places the erecting of a Colony, shall finde at the ende of seaven yeares occasion enough to use all his discretion: and, in the Interim all the content, rewards, gaines, and hopes will be necessar-

---

[12] Obstinancy.
[13] Anxiously.
[14] Duty.

ily required, to be given to the beginning, till it bee able to creepe, to stand, and goe, yet time enough to keepe it from running, for there is no feare it wil grow too fast, or ever to any thing; except libertie, profit, honor, and prosperitie there found, more binde the planters of those affaires, in devotion to effect it; then bondage, violence, tyranny, ingratitude, and such double dealing, as bindes free men to become slaves, and honest men turne knaves: which hath ever bin the ruine of the most popular commonweales; and is verie unlikelie ever well to begin in a new.

Who seeth not what is the greatest good of the Spanyard, but these new conclusions, in searching those unknowne parts of this unknowne world? By which meanes hee dives even into the verie secrets of all his Neighbours, and the most part of the world: and when the Portugale and Spanyard had found the East and West Indies; how many did condemn themselves, that did not accept of that honest offer of Noble Columbus?[15] who, upon our neglect, brought them to it, perswading our selves the world had no such places as they had found: and yet ever since wee finde, they still (from time to time) have found new Lands, new Nations, and trades, and still daily dooe finde both in Asia, Africa, Terra incognita,[16] and America; so that there is neither Soldier nor Mechanick,[17] from the Lord to the begger, but those parts afforde them all imploiment; and discharge their Native soile, of so many thousands of all sorts, that else, by their sloth, pride, and imperfections, would long ere this have troubled their neighbours, or have eaten the pride of Spaine it selfe.

Now he knowes little, that knowes not England may well spare many more people then Spaine, and is as well able to furnish them with all manner of necessaries. And seeing, for all they have, they cease not still to search for that they have not, and know not; It is strange we should be so dull, as not maintaine that which wee have, and pursue that wee knowe. Surely I am sure many would taste it ill, to bee abridged of the titles and honours of their predecessors: when if but truely they would judge themselves; looke how inferior they are to their noble vertues, so much they are unworthy of their honours and livings: which never were ordained for showes and shadowes, to maintaine idlenesse and vice; but to make them more able to abound in honor, by heroycall deeds of action, judgement, pietie, and vertue. What was it, They would not doe both in purse and person, for the good of the Commonwealth? which might move them presently to set out their spare kindred in these generous designes. Religion, above all things, should move us (especially the Clergie) if wee

[15] Bartholomew Columbus.
[16] Unknown, unexplored land.
[17] A person with a manual occupation.

were religious, to shewe our faith by our workes; in converting those poore salvages, to the knowledge of God, seeing what paines the Spanyards take to bring them to their adulterated faith.[18] Honor might move the Gentrie, the valiant, and industrious; and the hope and assurance of wealth, all; if wee were that we would seeme, and be accounted. Or be we so far inferior to other nations, or our spirits so far dejected, from our auncient predecessors, or our mindes so upon spoile, piracie, and such villany, as to serve the Portugall, Spanyard, Dutch, French, or Turke (as to the cost of Europe, too many dooe) rather than our God, our King, our Country, and our selves? excusing our idlenesse, and our base complaints, by want of imploiment; when heere is such choise of all sorts, and for all degrees, in the planting and discovering these North parts of America.

ADVERTISEMENTS FOR THE UNEXPERIENCED PLANTERS OF NEW ENGLAND

Many good religious devout men have made it a great question, as a matter in conscience, by what warrant they might goe to possesse those Countries, which are none of theirs, but the poore Salvages. Which poore curiosity will answer it selfe; for God did make the world to be inhabited with mankind, and to have his name knowne to all Nations, and from generation to generation: as the people increased they dispersed themselves into such Countries as they found most convenient. And here in Florida, Virginia, New-England, and Cannada, is more land than all the people in Christendome can manure, and yet more to spare than all the natives of those Countries can use and culturate.[19] And shall we here keepe such a coyle[20] for land, and at such great rents and rates, when there is so much of the world uninhabited, and as much more in other places, and as good, or rather better than any wee possesse, were it manured and used accordingly. If this be not a reason sufficient to such tender consciences; for a copper kettle and a few toyes, as beads and hatchets, they will sell you a whole Countrey; and for a small matter, their houses and the ground they dwell upon; but those of the Massachusets have resigned theirs freely.

---

[18] Most English Protestants, but especially the Puritans, felt that the rituals of the Roman Catholic church and even the Church of England interfered with the proper relationship between individuals and God.

[19] Cultivate.

[20] Coil, a noisy disturbance or turmoil.

Now the reasons for plantations are many; Adam and Eve did first begin this innocent worke to plant the earth to remaine to posterity, but not without labour, trouble, and industry: Noah and his family began againe the second plantation, and their seed as it still increased, hath still planted new Countries, and one Country another, and so the world to that estate it is; but not without much hazard, travell,[21] mortalities, discontents, and many disasters: had those worthy Fathers and their memorable off-spring not beene more diligent for us now in those ages, than wee are to plant that yet unplanted for after-livers. Had the seed of Abraham, our Saviour Christ Jesus and his Apostles, exposed themselves to no more dangers to plant the Gospell wee so much professe, than we, even we our selves had at this present beene as Salvages, and as miserable as the most barbarous Salvage, yet uncivilized. The Hebrewes, Lacedemonians,[22] the Goths, Grecians, Romans, and the rest, what was it they would not undertake to inlarge their Territories, inrich their subjects, and resist their enemies. Those that were the founders of those great Monarchies and their vertues, were no silvered idle golden Pharisies,[23] but industrious honest hearted Publicans,[24] they regarded more provisions and necessaries for their people, than jewels, ease and delight for themselves; riches was their servants, not their masters; they ruled as fathers, not as tyrants; their people as children, not as slaves; there was no disaster could discourage them; and let none thinke they incountered not with all manner of incumbrances, and what hath ever beene the worke of the best great Princes of the world, but planting of Countries, and civilizing barbarous and inhumane Nations to civility and humanity, whose eternall actions fils our histories with more honour than those that have wasted and consumed them by warres.

Lastly, the Portugals and Spaniards that first began plantations in this unknowne world of America till within this 140. yeares, whose everlasting actions before our eyes, will testifie our idlenesse and ingratitude to all posterity, and neglect of our duty and religion wee owe our God, our King, and Countrey, and want of charity to those poore Salvages, whose Countries we challenge, use, and possesse, except wee be but made to marre what our forefathers made, or but only tell what they did, or esteeme our selves too good to take the like paines where there is so much reason,

[21] Travail, hard work.
[22] Spartans.
[23] Self-righteous hypocrites. The term derives from an ancient Jewish sect distinguished by their strict observance of the law and their pretentions to superior sanctity.
[24] A tax gatherer in ancient Rome, but later referring to any collector of tribute or customs.

liberty, and action offers it selfe, having as much power and meanes as others: why should English men despaire and not doe so much as any? Was it vertue in those Heros to provide that doth maintaine us, and basenesse in us to doe the like for others to come? Surely no; then seeing wee are not borne for our selves but each to helpe other, and our abilities are much alike at the howre of our birth and minute of our death: seeing our good deeds or bad, by faith in Christs merits, is all wee have to carry our soules to heaven or hell: Seeing honour is our lives ambition, and our ambition after death, to have an honourable memory of our life: and seeing by no meanes wee would be abated of the dignitie and glorie of our predecessors, let us imitate their vertues to be worthily their successors, or at least not hinder, if not further them that would and doe their utmost and best endevour.

10

WILLIAM WOOD

New England's Prospect
1635

We know very little about William Wood, author of New England's Prospect, A True, Lively, and Experimentall Description of That Part of
America, Commonly Called New England, *a work that first appeared in
1634. Apparently he arrived in New England in 1629 and returned to
England four years later. It is possible that he returned again to Massachusetts Bay, since the records of the province note the existence of a William
Wood who lived in Saugus in 1635 and 1636, a William Wood who became a
founder of Sandwich in 1637, and a William Wood who died in Concord
about forty years later (in 1670 or 1671). Unlike the other promoters whose
writing appears in this book it is impossible to link the author of this tract to
any particular biographical details.*

Whoever he was, the Wood who wrote New England's Prospect *was a
talented and literate observer of early Massachusetts. As had become a
well-established custom among promoters by the early 1630s, Wood described
the natural resources of the region in great detail. He even wrote poems about
particular aspects of the regional flora and fauna; his verse about trees,
which begins with "Trees both in hills and plains in plenty be, / The
long-lived oak and mournful cypress tree," continues for twenty lines,
extolling the qualities of particular species. His prose often included precise
descriptions of the regional Indians, including the Pequots, Narragansetts,
and Mohawks, and their customs and beliefs. These passages make* New
England's Prospect *valuable because Wood, like Harriot and Smith, witnessed Indian practices in the years before widespread migration of colonists
displaced coastal groups and before the Pequot War (1637), the most notable
early conflict between Indians and colonists in New England. Though Wood
apparently spent little time among Indians himself, he used a strategy
common to writers of promotional materials about North America: he included the observations of others who had more experience. Fortunately
for modern readers, Wood found ample detail about mundane aspects of*

William Wood, *New England's Prospect,* ed. Alden T. Vaughan (Amherst: University of
Massachusetts Press, 1977).

*daily life, and his discussion of the lives of Indian women in New Eng-
land has allowed us rare insight into gender roles among America's natives.*

*Writing more in a descriptive than an overtly promotional tone, Wood
seems to have been striving for a level of objective reportage in his account.
His title page noted that the work intended to lay "downe that which may both
enrich the knowledge of the mind-travelling Reader, or benefit the future
Voyager." If this was the case, what impact could his description of Indians
have had on the potential migrants to New England? In what ways do
Wood's descriptions of America's peoples differ from those of Harriot? Do his
accounts of the Indians' government, religion, and social customs seem
realistic? What do his writings say about the roles of Indian men and
women? What can we learn about early colonist-Indian relations from
studying the "Small Nomenclator" that Wood appended to his work?*

Of Their Wondering at the First View of Any Strange Invention

These Indians being strangers to arts and sciences, and being un-
acquainted with the inventions that are common to civilized people, are
ravished with admiration at the first view of any such sight. They took the
first ship they saw for a walking island, the mast to be a tree, the sail white
clouds, and the discharging of ordnance[1] for lightning and thunder which
did much trouble them, but this thunder being over and this moving-island
steadied with an anchor, they manned out their canoes to go and pick
strawberries there. But being saluted by the way with a broadside, they
cried out, "What much hoggery,[2] so big walk, and so big speak, and by and
by kill"; which caused them to turn back, not daring to approach till they
were sent for.

They do much extol and wonder at the English for their strange
inventions, especially for a windmill which in their esteem was little less
than the world's wonder, for the strangeness of his whisking motion and
the sharp teeth biting the corn (as they term it) into such small pieces,
they were loath at the first to come near to his long arms, or to abide in so
tottering a tabernacle,[3] though now they dare go anywhere so far as they
have an English guide. The first plowman was counted little better than a
juggler: the Indians, seeing the plow tear up more ground in a day than

[1] Firearms.
[2] Hoggishness; i.e., brutishness.
[3] Dwelling.

their clamshells could scrape up in a month, desired to see the workmanship of it, and viewing well the coulter and share, perceiving it to be iron, told the plowman he was almost Abamacho,[4] almost as cunning as the Devil. But the fresh supplies of new and strange objects hath lessened their admiration and quickened their inventions and desire of practising such things as they see, wherein they express no small ingenuity and dexterity of wit, being neither furthered by art [n]or long experience.

It is thought they would soon learn any mechanical trades, having quick wits, understanding apprehensions, strong memories, with nimble inventions, and a quick hand in using of the ax or hatchet or such like tools. Much good might they receive from the English, and much might they benefit themselves, if they were not strong fettered in the chains of idleness; so as that they had rather starve than work, following no employments saving such as are sweetened with more pleasures and profit than pains or care, and this is indeed one of the greatest accusations that can be laid against them which lies but upon the men (the women being very industrious). But it may be hoped that good example and good instructions may bring them to a more industrious and provident course of life, for already, as they have learned much subtlety and cunning by bargaining with the English, so have they a little degenerated from some of their lazy customs and show themselves more industrious.

In a word, to set them out in their best colors, they be wise in their carriage, subtle in their dealings, true in their promise, honest in defraying of their debts, though poverty constrain them to be something long before. Some having died in the English debt had left beaver by order of will for their satisfaction. They be constant in friendship, merrily conceited[5] in discourse, not luxuriously abounding in youth nor dotingly forward in old age, many of them being much civilized since the English colonies were planted, though but little edified in religion. They frequent often the English churches where they will sit soberly, though they understand not such hidden mysteries. They do easily believe some of the history of the Bible, as the creation of the world, the making of man, with his fall. But come to tell them of a Saviour, with all the passages of the Gospel, and it exceeds so far their Indian belief that they will cry out *"Pocatnie"* (*id est,* is it possible?). Yet such is their conviction of the right way that when some English have come to their houses, victuals being offered them, forgetting to crave God's blessing upon the creatures received, they have been reproved by these which formerly never knew

---

[4] The devil.
[5] Intelligent or clever.

what calling upon God meant. Thus far for their natural disposition and qualities.

Of Their Kings' Government and Subjects' Obedience

Nor for the matter of government amongst them. It is the custom for their kings to inherit, the son always taking the kingdom after his father's death. If there be no son, then the queen rules; if no queen, the next to the blood-royal.[6] Who comes in otherwise is but counted an usurping intruder, and if his fair carriage bear him not out the better, they will soon unscepter him.

The kings have not many laws to command by, nor have they any annual revenues; yet commonly are they so either feared or beloved that half their subjects' estate is at their service and their persons at his command, by which command he is better known than by anything else. For though he hath no kingly robes to make him glorious in the view of his subjects, nor daily guards to secure his person, or court-like attendance, nor sumptuous palaces, yet do they yield all submissive subjection to him, accounting him their sovereign, going at his command and coming at his beck, not so much as expostulating the cause though it be in matters thwarting their wills, he being accounted a disloyal subject that will not effect what his prince commands.

Whosoever is known to plot treason or to lay violent hands on his lawful king is presently executed. Once a year he takes his progress, accompanied with a dozen of his best subjects, to view his country, to recreate[7] himself, and establish good order. When he enters into any of their houses, without any more compliment he is desired to sit down on the ground (for they use neither stools nor cushions), and after a little respite all that be present come in and sit down by him, one of his seniors pronouncing an oration gratulatory to his majesty for his love and the many good things they enjoy under his peaceful government.

A king of large dominions hath his viceroys, or inferior kings, under him to agitate his state affairs and keep his subjects in good decorum. Other officers there be, but how to distinguish them by name is something difficult. For their laws, as their evil courses come short of many other nations', so they have not so many laws, though they be not without some which they inflict upon notorious malefactors, as traitors to their prince, inhumane murtherers, and (some say) for adultery, but I cannot warrant it

[6] Many eastern woodlands Indians, including groups in New England, were matrilineal.
[7] Refresh or enliven.

for a truth. For theft, as they have nothing to steal worth the life of a man, therefore they have no law to execute for trivials, a subject being precious in the eye of his prince where men are so scarce. A malefactor having deserved death, being apprehended is brought before the king and some other of the wisest men, where they inquire out the original of a thing. After proceeding by aggravation of circumstances, he is found guilty, and being cast by the jury of their strict inquisition, he is condemned and executed on this manner: the executioner comes in, who blindfolds the party, sets him in the public view, and brains him with a tomahawk or club; which done, his friends bury him. Other means to restrain abuses they have none, saving admonition or reproof; no whippings, no prisons, stocks, bilboes,[8] or the like.

Of Their Marriages

Now to speak something of their marriages. The kings or great powwows, alias conjurers, may have two or three wives but seldom use it, men of ordinary rank having but one; which disproves the report that they had eight or ten wives apiece. When a man hath a desire to marry, he first gets the good will of the maid or widow; after, the consent of her friends for her part. And for himself, if he be at his own disposing, if the king will, the match is made, her dowry of wampompeag[9] paid, the king joins their hands with their hearts, never to part till death unless she prove a whore, for which they may (and some have) put away their wives, as may appear by a story.

There was one Abamoch married a wife, whom a long time he entirely loved above her deservings, for that she often in his absence entertained strangers, of which he was oftentimes informed by his neighbors. But he harboring no spark of jealousy, believed not their false informations (as he deemed them) being in a manner angry they should slander his wife, of whose constancy he was so strongly conceited.[10] A long time did her whorish glozing[11] and Siren-like tongue, with her subtle carriage, establish her in her husband's favor till fresh complaints caused him to cast about how to find out the truth and to prove his friends liars and his wife honest, or her a whore and his friends true. Whereupon he pretended a long journey to visit his friends, providing all accoutrements for a fortnight's journey, telling his wife it would be so long before she could expect his

---

[8] Iron bars with shackles for confining the feet.
[9] Wampum, originally small shells, later glass beads.
[10] Convinced.
[11] Flattery.

return, who outwardly sorrowed for his departure but inwardly rejoiced that she should enjoy the society of her old leman,[12] whom she sent for with expedition, not suspecting her husband's plot, who lay not many miles off in the woods; who, after their dishonest revelings, when they were in their midnight sleep, approaches the wigwam, enters the door, which was neither barred nor locked, makes a light to discover what he little suspected. But finding his friends' words to be true, he takes a good bastinado[13] in his hand, brought for the same purpose, dragging him by the hair from his usurped bed, so lamentably beating him that his battered bones and bruised flesh made him a fitter subject for some skillful surgeon than the lovely object of a lustful strumpet.[14] Which done, he put away his wife, exposing her to the courtesy of strangers for her maintenance, that so courtesan-like had entertained a stranger into her bosom.

Of Their Worship, Invocations, and Conjurations

Now of their worships. As it is natural to all mortals to worship something, so do these people, but exactly to describe to whom their worship is chiefly bent is very difficult. They acknowledge especially two: Ketan who is their good god, to whom they sacrifice (as the ancient heathen did to Ceres)[15] after their garners[16] be full with a good crop; upon this god likewise they invoke for fair weather, for rain in time of drought, and for the recovery of their sick.

But if they do not hear them, then they verify the old verse, *flectere si nequeo superos, acharonta movebo,*[17] their powwows betaking themselves to their exorcisms and necromantic[18] charms by which they bring to pass strange things, if we may believe the Indians who report of one Passaconaway that he can make the water burn, the rocks move, the trees dance, metamorphise himself into a flaming man. But it may be objected, this is but *deceptio visus.*[19] He will therefore do more, for in winter, when there is no green leaves to be got, he will burn an old one to ashes, and putting those into the water produce a new green leaf which you shall not only see but substantially handle and carry away, and make of a dead snake's skin a

[12] Lover.
[13] A stick or staff.
[14] Prostitute.
[15] Roman goddess of agriculture.
[16] Storehouses used for grain.
[17] A passage from Vergil's *Aeneid* meaning "If I cannot sway the gods above, I'll stir up Hell." See Alden Vaughan's edition of Wood's *New England's Prospect,* 100, n. 45.
[18] Related to the telling of the future by communication with the dead.
[19] An illusion.

living snake, both to be seen, felt, and heard. This I write but on the report of the Indians, who constantly affirm stranger things.

But to make manifest that by God's permission, through the Devil's help, their charms are of force to produce effects of wonderment, an honest gentleman related a story to me, being an eyewitness of the same: a powwow having a patient with the stump of some small tree run through his foot, being past the cure of his ordinary surgery, betook himself to his charms, and being willing to show his miracle before the English stranger, he wrapped a piece of cloth about the foot of the lame man [and] upon that wrapping a beaver skin through which he — laying his mouth to the beaver skin — by his sucking charms he brought out the stump which he spat into a tray of water, returning the foot as whole as its fellow in a short time.

The manner of their action in their conjuration is thus: the parties that are sick or lame being brought before them, the powwow sitting down, the rest of the Indians giving attentive audience to his imprecations and invocations, and after the violent expression of many a hideous bellowing and groaning, he makes a stop, and then all the auditors with one voice utter a short canto.[20] Which done, the powwow still proceeds in his invocations, sometimes roaring like a bear, other times groaning like a dying horse, foaming at the mouth like a chased boar, smiting on his naked breast and thighs with such violence as if he were mad. Thus will he continue sometimes half a day, spending his lungs, sweating out his fat, and tormenting his body in this diabolical worship. Sometimes the Devil for requital of their worship recovers the party, to nuzzle them up in their devilish religion. In former time he was wont to carry away their wives and children, because he would drive them to these matins[21] to fetch them again to confirm their belief of this, his much desired authority over them. But since the English frequented those parts, they daily fall from his colors,[22] relinquishing their former fopperies,[23] and acknowledge our God to be supreme. They acknowledge the power of the Englishman's God, as they call him, because they could never yet have power by their conjurations to damnify the English either in body or goods; and besides, they say he is a good God that sends them so many good things, so much good corn, so many cattle, temperate rains, fair seasons, which they likewise are the better for since the arrival of the English, the times and seasons being much altered in seven or eight years, freer from lightning and

[20] A song or ballad.
[21] A monastic hour; morning prayer. Vaughan suggests that Wood is referring to "devil worship" (101, n. 47).
[22] Authority, influence.
[23] Foolishness or folly.

thunder, long droughts, sudden and tempestuous dashes of rain, and lamentable cold winters.

Of Their Wars

Of their wars: their old soldiers being swept away by the plague which was very rife amongst them about fourteen years ago, and resting themselves secure under the English protection, they do not now practice anything in martial feats worth observation, saving that they make themselves forts to fly into if the enemies should unexpectedly assail them. These forts some be forty or fifty foot square, erected of young timber trees ten or twelve foot high, rammed into the ground, with undermining within, the earth being cast up for their shelter against the dischargements of their enemies, having loopholes to send out their winged messengers, which often deliver their sharp and bloody embassies in the tawny sides of their naked assailants, who wanting butting-rams and battering ordnances to command at distance, lose their lives by their too near approachments.

These [people] use no other weapons in war than bows and arrows, saving that their captains have long spears on which, if they return conquerors, they carry the heads of their chief enemies that they slay in the wars, it being the custom to cut off their heads, hands, and feet to bear home to their wives and children as true tokens of their renowned victory. When they go to their wars, it is their custom to paint their faces with diversity of colors, some being all black as jet, some red, some half red and half black, some black and white, others spotted with diverse kinds of colors, being all disguised to their enemies to make them more terrible to their foes, putting on likewise their rich jewels, pendants, and wampompeag, to put them in mind they fight not only for their children, wives, and lives, but likewise for their goods, lands, and liberties. Being thus armed with this warlike paint, the antic[24] warriors make towards their enemies in a disordered manner, without any soldier-like marching or warlike postures, being deaf to any word of command, ignorant of falling off or falling on, of doubling ranks or files, but let fly their winged shaftments without either fear or wit. Their artillery being spent, he that hath no arms to fight, finds legs to run away. . . .

Of Their Language

Of their language, which is only peculiar to themselves, not inclining to any of the refined tongues: some have thought they might be of the dispersed

[24] Grotesque or bizarre.

Jews because some of their words be near unto the Hebrew, but by the same rule they may conclude them to be of some of the gleanings of all nations because they have words which sound after the Greek, Latin, French, and other tongues. Their language is hard to learn, few of the English being able to speak any of it, or capable of the right pronunciation, which is the chief grace of their tongue. They pronounce much after the dipthongs, excluding L and R, which in our English tongue they pronounce with as much difficulty as most of the Dutch do T and H, calling a lobster a *nobstann.*

Every country do something differ in their speech, even as our northern people do from the southern, and western from them; especially the Tarrenteens, whose tongues run so much upon R that they wharle[25] much in pronunciation. When any ships come near the shore, they demand whether they be King Charles his Tories, with such a rumbling sound as if one were beating an unbraced drum. In serious discourse our southern Indians use seldom any short colloquiums but speak their minds at large without any interjected interruptions from any, the rest giving diligent audience to his utterance. Which done, some or other returns him as long an answer. They love not to speak *multa sed multum;*[26] seldom are their words and their deeds strangers. According to the matter in discourse, so are their acting gestures in their expressions.

One of the English preachers, in a special good intent of doing good to their souls, hath spent much time in attaining to their language, wherein he is so good a proficient that he can speak to their understanding and they to his, much loving and respecting him for his love and counsel. It is hoped that he may be an instrument of good amongst them.[27] They love any man that can utter his mind in their words, yet are they not a little proud that they can speak the English tongue, using it as much as their own when they meet with such as can understand it, puzzling stranger Indians, which sometimes visit them from more remote places, with an unheard language.

Of Their Deaths, Burials, and Mourning

Although the Indians be of lusty and healthful bodies, not experimentally knowing the catalogue of those health-wasting diseases which are incident

[25] According to Vaughan, this meant "pronounce with a guttural sound" (110, n. 62).

[26] "Many but much." According to Vaughan, Wood meant to suggest "they say much in a few words" (110, n. 63).

[27] Wood here is presumably referring to Roger Williams, perhaps the most important English missionary working among New England Indians during the early seventeenth century (ibid, n. 64).

to other countries, as fevers, pleurisies,[28] callentures,[29] agues,[30] obstructions, consumptions, subfumigations,[31] convulsions, apoplexies,[32] dropsies,[33] gouts, stones, toothaches, pox, measles, or the like, but spin out the thread of their days to a fair length, numbering threescore, fourscore, some a hundred years, before the world's universal summoner cite them to the craving grave.

But the date of their life expired, and death's arrestment seizing upon them, all hope of recovery being past, then to behold and hear their throbbing sobs and deep-fetched sighs, their grief-wrung hands and tear-bedewed cheeks, their doleful cries, would draw tears from adamantine[34] eyes that be but spectators of their mournful obsequies. The glut of their grief being past, they commit the corpses of their deceased friends to the ground, over whose grave is for a long time spent many a briny tear, deep groan, and Irish-like howlings,[35] continuing annual mournings with a black, stiff paint on their faces. These are the mourners without hope, yet do they hold the immortality of the never-dying soul that it shall pass to the southwest Elysium, concerning which their Indian faith jumps much with the Turkish Alcoran,[36] holding it to be a kind of paradise wherein they shall everlastingly abide, solacing themselves in odoriferous gardens, fruitful corn fields, green meadows, bathing their tawny hides in the cool streams of pleasant rivers, and shelter themselves from heat and cold in the sumptuous palaces framed by the skill of nature's curious contrivement; concluding that neither care nor pain shall molest them but that nature's bounty will administer all things with a voluntary contribution from the overflowing storehouse of their Elysian Hospital, at the portal whereof, they say, lies a great dog whose churlish snarlings deny a *pax intrantibus*[37] to unworthy intruders. Wherefore it is their custom to bury with them their bows and arrows and good store of their wampompeag and

---

[28] Inflammation of the membrane lining the thorax and enveloping the lungs.

[29] Calenture was a disease characterized by delirium and hallucinations, afflicting sailors in the tropics.

[30] Fevers.

[31] According to Vaughan, this is an obsolete form of *suffumigation*, but the meaning "is not clear because subfumigation (fumigation from below) was a therapeutic treatment rather than a disease or ailment" (111, n. 65).

[32] Strokes.

[33] Swelling in body tissue.

[34] Immovable, impregnable.

[35] Presumably a pejorative reference to Irish Catholics and the fact that many English people of this period considered the Irish rude barbarians.

[36] The Koran.

[37] "Peace to those entering."

mowhacheis;[38] the one to affright that affronting Cerberus,[39] the other to purchase more immense prerogatives in their paradise. For their enemies and loose livers, whom they account unworthy of this imaginary happiness, they say that they pass to the infernal dwellings of Abamacho, to be tortured according to the fictions of the ancient heathen.

Of Their Women, Their Dispositions, Employments, Usage by Their Husbands, Their Apparel, and Modesty

To satisfy the curious eye of women readers, who otherwise might think their sex forgotten or not worthy a record, let them peruse these few lines wherein they may see their own happiness, if weighed in the woman's balance of these ruder Indians who scorn the tutorings of their wives or to admit them as their equals — though their qualities and industrious deservings may justly claim the preeminence and command better usage and more conjugal esteem, their persons and features being every way correspondent, their qualifications more excellent, being more loving, pitiful, and modest, mild, provident, and laborious than their lazy husbands.

Their employments be many: first their building of houses, whose frames are formed like our garden arbors, something more round, very strong and handsome, covered with close-wrought mats of their own weaving which deny entrance to any drop of rain, though it come both fierce and long, neither can the piercing north wind find a cranny through which he can convey his cooling breath. They be warmer than our English houses. At the top is a square hole for the smoke's evacuation, which in rainy weather is covered with a pluver.[40] These be such smoky dwellings that when there is good fires they are not able to stand upright, but lie all along under the smoke, never using any stools or chairs, it being as rare to see an Indian sit on a stool at home as it is strange to see an Englishman sit on his heels abroad. Their houses are smaller in the summer when their families be dispersed by reason of heat and occasions. In winter they make some fifty or threescore foot long, forty or fifty men being inmates under one roof. And as is their husbands' occasion, these poor tectonists[41] are often troubled like snails to carry their houses on their backs, sometime to fishing places, other times to hunting places, after that to a planting place where it abides the longest.

[38] Indian gold.
[39] The three-headed dog that guarded Hades in Greek and Roman myth.
[40] According to Vaughan, "Wood apparently meant a rain-cover" (112, n. 70).
[41] Builders.

Another work is their planting of corn, wherein they exceed our English husbandmen, keeping it so clear with their clamshell hoes as if it were a garden rather than a corn field, not suffering a choking weed to advance his audacious head above their infant corn or an undermining worm to spoil his spurns. Their corn being ripe they gather it, and drying it hard in the sun convey it to their barns, which be great holes digged in the ground in form of a brass pot, sealed with rinds of trees, wherein they put their corn, covering it from the inquisitive search of their gourmandizing husbands who would eat up both their allowed portion and reserved seed if they knew where to find it. But our hogs having found a way to unhinge their barn doors and rob their garners, they are glad to implore their husbands' help to roll the bodies of trees over their holes to prevent those pioneers whose thievery they as much hate as their flesh.

Another of their employments is their summer processions to get lobsters for their husbands, wherewith they bait their hooks when they go afishing for bass or codfish. This is an everyday's walk, be the weather cold or hot, the waters rough or calm. They must dive sometimes over head and ears for a lobster, which often shakes them by their hands with a churlish nip and bids them adieu. The tide being spent, they trudge home two or three miles with a hundredweight of lobsters at their backs, and if none, a hundred scowls meet them at home and a hungry belly for two days after. Their husbands having caught any fish, they bring it in their boats as far as they can by water and there leave it; as it was their care to catch it, so it must be their wives' pains to fetch it home, or fast. Which done, they must dress it and cook it, dish it, and present it, see it eaten over their shoulders; and their loggerships[42] having filled their paunches, their sweet lullabies scramble for their scraps. In the summer these Indian women, when lobsters be in their plenty and prime, they dry them to keep for winter, erecting scaffolds in the hot sunshine, making fires likewise underneath them (by whose smoke the flies are expelled) till the substance remain hard and dry. In this manner they dry bass and other fishes without salt, cutting them very thin to dry suddenly before the flies spoil them or the rain moist them, having a special care to hang them in their smoky houses in the night and dankish weather.

In summer they gather flags,[43] of which they make mats for houses, and hemp and rushes, with dyeing stuff of which they make curious baskets with intermixed colors and protractures[44] of antic imagery. These

[42] Sluggards, lazy or idle persons.
[43] Reeds or rushes, North American cattails.
[44] Drawings.

baskets be of all sizes from a quart to a quarter,[45] in which they carry their luggage. In winter they are their husband's caterers, trudging to the clam banks for their belly timber, and their porters to lug home their venison which their laziness exposes to the wolves till they impose it upon their wives' shoulders. They likewise sew their husbands' shoes and weave coats of turkey feathers, besides all their ordinary household drudgery which daily lies upon them, so that a big belly hinders no business, nor a childbirth takes much time, but the young infant being greased and sooted,[46] wrapped in a beaver skin, bound to his good behavior with his feet up to his bum upon a board two foot long and one foot broad, his face exposed to all nipping weather, this little papoose travels about with his bare-footed mother to paddle in the icy clam banks after three or four days of age have sealed his passboard[47] and his mother's recovery.

For their carriage it is very civil, smiles being the greatest grace of their mirth; their music is lullabies to quiet their children, who generally are as quiet as if they had neither spleen or lungs. To hear one of these Indians unseen, a good ear might easily mistake their untaught voice for the warbling of a well-tuned instrument, such command have they of their voices.

These women's modesty drives them to wear more clothes than their men, having always a coat of cloth or skins wrapped like a blanket about their loins, reaching down to their hams, which they never put off in company. If a husband have a mind to sell his wife's beaver petticoat, as sometimes he doth, she will not put it off until she have another to put on. Commendable is their mild carriage and obedience to their husbands, notwithstanding all this—their [husband's] customary churlishness and savage inhumanity—not seeming to delight in frowns or offering to word it with their lords, not presuming to proclaim their female superiority to the usurping of the least title of their husband's charter, but rest themselves content under their helpless condition, counting it the woman's portion.

Since the English arrival, comparison hath made them miserable, for seeing the kind usage of the English to their wives, they do as much condemn their husbands for unkindness and commend the English for their love, as their husbands—commending themselves for their wit in keeping their wives industrious—do condemn the English for their folly in spoiling

---

[45] Eight bushels; see Vaughan, 114, n. 75.

[46] Stained dark.

[47] Passport. As Vaughan notes, "Wood apparently here used a whimsical allusion to the infant's entrance into human society" (114, n. 77).

good working creatures. These women resort often to the English houses, where *pares cum paribus congregatae,*[48] in sex I mean, they do somewhat ease their misery by complaining and seldom part without a relief. If her husband come to seek for his squaw and begin to bluster, the English woman betakes her to her arms, which are the warlike ladle and the scalding liquors, threatening blistering to the naked runaway, who is soon expelled by such liquid comminations.[49]

In a word, to conclude this woman's history, their love to the English hath deserved no small esteem, ever presenting them something that is either rare or desired, as strawberries, hurtleberries, raspberries, gooseberries, cherries, plums, fish, and other such gifts as their poor treasury yields them. But now it may be that this relation of the churlish and inhumane behavior of these ruder Indians towards their patient wives may confirm some in the belief of an aspersion which I have often heard men cast upon the English there, as if they should learn of the Indians to use their wives in the like manner and to bring them to the same subjection—as to sit on the lower hand and to carry water and the like drudgery. But if my own experience may out-balance an ill-grounded scandalous rumor, I do assure you, upon my credit and reputation, that there is no such matter, but the women find there as much love, respect, and ease as here in old England. I will not deny but that some poor people may carry their own water. And do not the poorer sort in England do the same, witness your London tankard bearers and your country cottagers? But this may well be known to be nothing but the rancorous venom of some that bear no good will to the plantation. For what need they carry water, seeing everyone hath a spring at his door or the sea by his house?

Thus much for the satisfaction of women, touching this entrenchment upon their prerogative, as also concerning the relation of these Indian squaws.

"A SMALL NOMENCLATOR" OF THE INDIAN LANGUAGE

Because many have desired to hear some of the natives' language, I have here inserted a small nomenclator, with the names of their chief kings, rivers, months and days, whereby such as have insight into the tongues may know to what language it is most inclining; and such as desire it as an unknown language only, may reap delight, if they can get no profit.

[48]"Equals gathered together with equals."
[49]Threats of divine punishment or vengeance.

A
Aberginian—an Indian
Abamocho—the Devil
Aunum—a dog
Ausupp—a raccoon
Au so hau nouc hoc—lobster
Assawog—will you play
A saw upp—tomorrow
Ascoscoi—green
Ausomma petuc quanocke—give
   me some bread
Appepes naw aug—when I see it
   I will tell you my mind
Anno ke nugge—a sieve
An nu ocke—a bed
Autchu wompocke—today
Appause—the morn
Ascom quom pauputchim—thanks
   be given to God

B
Bequoquo—the head
Bisquant—the shoulderbones

C
Chesco kean—you lie
Commouton kean—you steal
Cram—to kill
Chickachava—*osculari podicem*[50]
Cowimms—sleeps
Cocam—the navel
Cos—the nails
Conomma—a spoon
Cossaquot—bow and arrows
Cone—the sun
Cotattup—I drink to you
Coetop—will you drink tobacco
Connucke sommona—it is almost
   night
Connu—good night to you
Cowompanu sin—God morrow
Coepot—ice

D
Dottaguck—the backbone
Docke taugh he necke—what is
   your name

E
Et chossucke—a knife
Eat chumnis—Indian corn
Eans causuacke—four fathoms
Easu tommoc quocke—half a skin
   of beaver
Epimetsis—much good may your
   meat do you

F is never used.

G
Gettoquaset—the great toe
Genehuncke—the forefinger
Gettoquacke—the knees
Gettoquun—the knuckles
Gettoquan—the thumb
Gegnewaw og—let me see

H
Haha—yes
Hoc—the body
Hamucke—almost
Hub hub hub—come come come
Haddo quo dunna moquonash—
   where did you buy that
Haddogoe weage—who lives here

I
Isattonaneise—the bread
Icattop—faint with hunger
Icattoquam—very sleepy

K
Kean—I
Keisseanchacke—back of the hand
Ksitta—it hurts me

[50] Vaughan notes that a 1639 edition of Wood's book contains as translation the "blunt Anglo-Saxon: 'kisse my assehole' " (118, n. 81).

Kawkenog wampompeage — let me
    see money
Kagmatcheu — will you eat meat
Ketottug — a whetstone
Kenie — very sharp
Kettotanese — lend me money
Kekechoi — much pain

L is not used.

M

Matchet — it is naught
Mattamoi — to die
Mitchin — meat
Misquantum — very angry
Mauncheake — be gone
Matta — no
Meseig — hair
Mamanock — the eyebrees[51]
Matchanne — the nose
Mattone — the lips
Mepeiteis — the teeth
Mattickeis — the shoulders
Mettosowset — the little toe
Metosaunige — the little finger
Misquish — the veins
Mohoc — the waist
Menisowhock — the genitals
Mocossa — the black of the nail
Matchanni — very sick
Monacus — bows and arrows
Manehops — sit down
Monakinne — a coat
Mawcus sinnus — a pair of shoes
Matchemauquot — it stinketh
Muskanai — a bone
Menota — a basket
Meatchis — be merry
Mawpaw — it snows
Mawnaucoi — very strong
Mutcheou — a very poor man
Monosketenog — what's this
Mouskett — the breech

Matchet wequon — very blunt
Matta ka tau caushana — will you
    not trade
Mowhacheis — Indian gold

N

Nancompees — a boy
Nickesquaw — a maid
Nean — you
Nippe — water
Nasamp — pottage
Nota — six
Nisquan — the elbow
Noenaset — the third toe
Nahenan — a turkey
Niccone — a blackbird
Naw naunidge — the middle finger
Napet — the arm
Nitchicke — the hand
Notoquap — the skin
Nogcus — the heart
Nobpaw nocke — the breastbone
Nequaw — the thighs
Netop — a friend
Nonmia — give me
Noeicantop — how do you
Nawhaw nissis — farewell
Noei pauketan — by and by kill
Nenetah ha — I'll fight with you
Noei comquocke — a codfish
Nepaupe — stand by
No ottut — a great journey
Necautauh hau — no such matter
Noewamma — he laugheth
Noeshow — a father
Nitka — a mother
Netchaw — a brother
Notonquous — a kinsman
Nenomous — a kinswoman
Nau mau nais — my son
Taunais — my daughter
No einshom — give me corn
Nemnis — take it

[51] Eyebrows.

Nenimma nequitta ta auchu—give me a span of anything
Nees nis ca su acke—two fathom
Notchumoi—a little strong
Negacawgh hi—lend me
Nebuks quam—adieu
Noe winyah—come in
Naut seam—much weary
Noe wammaw ause—I love you
Net noe whaw missu—a man of a middle stature

O

Ottucke—a deer
Occone—a deerskin
Oquan—the heel
Ottump—a bow
Ottommaocke—tobacco
Ottannapeake—the chin
Occotucke—the throat
Occasu—half a quarter
Unquagh saw au—you are cunning
Ontoquos—a wolf

P

Pow-wow—a conjurer or wizard
Petta sinna—give me a pipe of tobacco
Pooke—colt's foot
Pappouse—a child
Petucquanocke—bread
Picke—a pipe
Ponesanto—make a fire
Papowne—winter
Pequas—a fox
Pausochu—a little journey
Peamissin—a little
Peacumshis—work hard
Pokitta—smoke
Petogge—a bag
Paucasn—a quarter
Pausawniscosu—half a fathom
Peunctaumocke—much pray
Pesissu—a little man
Pausepissoi—the sun is rising

Pouckshaa—it is broken
Poebugketaas—you burn
Poussu—a big-bellied woman

Q

Quequas nummos—what cheer
Quequas nim—it is almost day
Quog quosh—make haste
Quenobpuuncke—a stool
Quenops—be quiet

R is never used.

S

Sagamore—a king
Sachem—idem
Sannup—a man
Squaw—a woman
Squitta—a fire spark
Suggig—a bass
Seasicke—a rattlesnake
Shannucke—a squirrel
Skesicos—the eyes
Sickeubecke—the neck
Supskinge—the wrist bones
Socottocanus—the breastbone
Squehincke—blood
Siccaw quant—the hams
Sis sau causke—the shins
Suppiske—ankle bones
Seat—the foot
Seaseap—a duck
Suckis suacke—a clam
Sequan—the summer
Soekepup—he will bite
Sis—come out
Squi—red
Swanscaw suacko—three fathoms
Sawawampeage—very weak
Succomme—I will eat you
Sasketupe—a great man

T

Taubut ne an hee—thanks heartily
Tantacum—beat him

Tap in — go in
Titta — I cannot tell
Tahanyah — what news
Tonagus — the ears
Tannicke — a cranny
Thaw — the calf of the leg
Tahaseat — the sole of the foot
Tasseche quonunck — the instep
Tonokete naum — whither go you
Tannissin may — which is the way
Tunketappin — where live you
Tonocco wam — where have you been
Tasis — a pair of stockings
Tockucke — a hatchet
Towwow — a sister
Tom maushew — a husband
Tookesin — enough sleep
Titto kean I catoquam — do you nod and sleep
Tau kequam — very heavy
Tauh coi — it is very cold

V [interchangeable with "U"]
Vkepemanous — the breastbone
Unkesheto — will you truck

W
Wampompeage — Indian money
Winnet — very good
Web — a wife
Wigwam — a house

Wawmott — enough
Whenan — the tongue
Whauksis — a fox
Wawpatucke — a goose
Wawpiske — the belly
Whoe nuncke — a ditch
Wappinne — the wind
Wawtom — understand you
Wompey — white
Wa aoy — the sun is down
Waacoh — the day breaks
Wekemawquot — it smells sweet
Weneikinne — it is very handsome
Whissu hochuck — the kettle boileth
Waawnew — you have lost your way
Woenaunta — it is a warm summer
Wompoca — tomorrow
Wawmauseu — an honest man
Weneicu — a rich man
Weitagcone — a clear day
Wawnauco — yesterday

X [is] never used.

Y
Yeips — sit down
Yaus — the sides
Yaugh — there
Yough yough — now
Yoakes — lice

THE NUMBER OF 20

1	A quit	6	Ocquinta	11	Apponna quit	16	Apponaquinta
2	Nees	7	Enotta	12	Apponees	17	Apponenotta
3	Nis	8	Sonaske	13	Apponis	18	Apponsonask
4	Yoaw	9	Assaquoquin	14	Appoyoaw	19	Apponasquoq
5	Abbona	10	Piocke	15	Apponabonna	20	Neenisschick

THE INDIANS COUNT THEIR TIME BY NIGHTS
AND NOT BY DAYS, AS FOLLOWETH

Sawup, 1 sleeps
Isoqunnocquock, 2 sleeps

Sucqunnocquocke, 3 sleeps
Yoawqunnocquock, 4 sleeps

Abonetta ta sucoqunnocquock, 5 sleeps
Nequitta ta sucqunnocquock, 6 sleeps
Enotta ta sucqunnocquock, 7 sleeps

Soesicta sucqunnocquock, 8 sleeps
Pausa quoquin sucqunnocquock, 9 sleeps
Pawquo qunnocquock, 10 sleeps

HOW THEY CALL THEIR MONTHS

A quit-appause, 1 months
Nees-appause, 2 months
Nis-appause, 3 months
Yoaw appause, 4 months
Abbonna appause, 5 months
Nequit appause, 6 months
Enotta appause, 7 months
Sonaske appause, 8 months
Assaquoquin appause, 9 months
Piocke appause, 10 months
Appona quit appause, 11 months
Appon nees appause, 12 months
Appon nis appause, 13 months
Appon yoaw appause, 14 months
Nap nappona appause, 15 months
Nap napocquint appause, 16 months

Nap nap enotta appause, 17 months
Napsoe sicke appause, 18 months
Nappawsoquoquin appause, 19 months
Neesnischicke appause, 20 months
Neesnischicke appon a quit appause, 21 months
Neesnischick apponees appause, 22 months
Neesnischick apponis appause, 23 months
Neesnischick appo yoaw appause, 24 months

THE NAMES OF THE INDIANS AS THEY BE DIVIDED INTO SEVERAL COUNTRIES

Tarrenteens	Aberginians	Pequants	Connectacuts
Churchers	Narragansets	Nipnets	Mowhacks

THE NAMES OF SAGAMORES[52]

Woenohaquahham—Anglice[53] King John
Montowompate—Anglice King James
Mausquonomend—Igowam sagamore
Chickkatawbut—Naponset sagamore
Nepawhamis, Nannoponnacund, Asteco, Nattonanite, Assotomowite, Noenotchuock

Nassawwhonan, Woesemagen—Two sagamores of Nipust
Canonicus—Narragansett sagamore
Osomeagen—Sagamore of the Pequants [Pequots]
Kekut—Petchutacut sagamore
Pissacannua—A sagamore and most noted necromancer
Sagamores to the East and Northeast bearing rule amongst the Churchers and Tarrenteens

[52] Chiefs.
[53] English.

THE NAMES OF THE MOST NOTED HABITATIONS

Merrimack
Igowam
Igoshaum
Chobocco *Anglice*
Nahumkeake — Salem
Saugus
Swampscot
Nahant
Winnisimmet
Mishaum
Mishaumut — Charlestown
Massachusetts — Boston
Mistick
Pigsgusset — Watertown
Naponset
Matampan — Dorchester
Pawtuxet — Plymouth

Wessaguscus
Conihosset
Mannimeed
Soewampset
Situate
Amuskeage
Pemmiquid
Saketehoc
Piscataqua
Cannibek
Penopscot
Pantoquid
Nawquot
Musketoquid
Nipnet
Whawcheusets

AT WHAT PLACES BE RIVERS OF NOTE

Cannibeck River
Merrimacke River
Tchobocco River
Saugus River
Mistick River
Mishaum River
Naponset River

Wessaguscus River
Luddams Ford
Narragansets River
Musketoquid River
Hunniborne River
Connectacut River

FINIS

Chronology of Exploration
and Colonization in the Americas

1000(?)–1500(?): Norse explorers colonize the North Atlantic, beginning with Iceland and then moving to Greenland and "Vinland," present-day Newfoundland.

1066: The Normans cross the English Channel and conquer England; a century later the Anglo-Normans cross the Irish Sea in the first English effort to colonize Ireland.

1492: Christopher Columbus, sailing west to find the East, lands in the Caribbean.

1493: Pope Alexander VI issues the bull (decree) of the Donacion, splitting the Western Hemisphere between Spain and Portugal.

1494: Spain and Portugal sign the Treaty of Tordesillas, giving Portugal rights to all land east of an imaginary line to the west of the Azores and Spain the possession of all land to the west of that line. The treaty gave Portugal the rights to what is now Brazil.

1497–98: John Cabot sails from Bristol, England, to the Western Hemisphere, but the English do not attempt to colonize North America for almost another century; English fishermen continue to sail the North Atlantic for decades.

1516: Thomas More publishes *The Best State of a Commonwealth and the New Island of Utopia.*

1519: Martin Luther breaks from the Catholic church in Germany and initiates the Reformation, a movement that leads to the development of Protestant Christianity.

1521: Hernando Cortés leads the Spanish victory over Montezuma and the Aztecs in Mexico City.

1530: Peter Martyr publishes a complete edition of *De Orbe Novo,* an account of the Americas based on interviews with Spanish explorers.

1533: Henry VIII breaks from the Catholic church and divorces Catherine of Aragon, thereby starting the Reformation in England.

1534–41:   Explorer Jacques Cartier sails up the St. Lawrence River and begins France's efforts to claim part of the Western Hemisphere.

1552:   Bartolomé de Las Casas publishes his *Short Account of the Destruction of the Indies,* recounting the sufferings of the indigenous peoples of the Americas who encountered the Spanish.

1558:   Accession of Elizabeth I to the English throne.

1560s: Elizabeth tries to conquer Ireland.

1570:   English population approximately 3.25 million.

1582:   Richard Hakluyt the younger publishes *Divers Voyages Touching the Discovery of America and the Ilands Adjacent.*

1583:   Sir Humphrey Gilbert, previously active in the English colonization of Ireland, is lost at sea on his return from Newfoundland; one of his associates, George Peckham, publishes his *True Reporte of the Late Discoveries . . . by . . . Sir Humphrey Gilbert* in an effort to sustain interest in the colonization of northeastern North America.

1584:   Richard Hakluyt the younger writes the "Discourse on Western Planting," a tract that circulates among English officials but is not published for almost three hundred years.

1584–1590:   Under the leadership of Sir Walter Ralegh, the English attempt to establish a colony in Roanoke off the coast of modern-day North Carolina. In 1584 two Carolina Algonquian Indians, Manteo and Wanchese, visit England. The last English colonists travel to Roanoke in 1587; by the time the next group arrives, in 1590, the entire colony has disappeared.

1585:   Richard Hakluyt the elder publishes "Inducements to the Liking of the Voyage Intended towards Virginia in 40. and 42. Degrees."

1587:   Richard Hakluyt the younger publishes the first edition of his *Principall Navigations;* he publishes a three-volume, expanded edition between 1598 and 1600.

1588:   An outnumbered English fleet defeats the Spanish Armada, thereby opening the Atlantic to more extensive colonization efforts.

1588:   Thomas Harriot's *A Briefe and True Report of the New Found Land of Virginia,* describing the resources and peoples of the Carolina coast, appears in England; two years later the next edition of the book, containing Theodore de Bry's engravings based on John White's paintings, provides Europeans with pictures of America's natives.

1595:   Ralegh makes his first visit to Guiana; the next year he publishes *The Discovery of the Large, Rich, and Beautiful Empire of Guiana.*

1600:   English population tops 4 million.

1603:   Queen Elizabeth dies; James I accedes to the English throne.

1607:   The Virginia Company sends 144 men and boys to establish James-town, near Chesapeake Bay, which becomes the first permanent English settlement in North America. By the end of the seventeenth century, tens of thousands of English men and women, most of them indentured servants, migrate from England to the Chesapeake region to work in the tobacco industry.

1609:   Henry Hudson sails up the river that now bears his name.

1610:   The Virginia Company publishes *A True Declaration of the Estate of the Colonie in Virginia* in an effort to counter the bleak reports emanating from the Chesapeake settlement.

1611:   William Shakespeare's *The Tempest* is performed in England.

1616:   Captain John Smith publishes *A Description of New England.*

1618:   Ralegh is executed for his efforts to establish an English colony in Guiana.

1620:   English Puritans establish their first settlement in New England at Plymouth.

1622:   A group of Powhatan Indians under the leadership of Opechan- canough launch an attack on colonists in Jamestown; the English quickly retaliate.

1624:   The Dutch begin the colonization of New Amsterdam on Manhattan.

1625:   Accession of Charles I to English throne.

1625:   George Percy, one of the early leaders of the colonization effort in the Chesapeake region, publishes his diary, which describes the difficulties facing the first colonists.

1630:   Establishment of Massachusetts Bay colony and the beginnings of the Great Migration of Puritans to New England; by 1642, when the large waves of migration end, approximately twenty-one thousand English men and women have crossed the Atlantic. A year before the establishment of the colony, Governor John Winthrop writes his "Reasons to Be Considered," in which he justifies seizing lands from local Indians and encourages cautious Puritans to join the venture.

1631:   Captain John Smith publishes his *Advertisements for the Un-experienced Planters of New England, or Any Where,* his last work and his most important statement on the English colonization of North America.

1634:   Establishment of an English colony in Maryland.

1634:   William Wood publishes the first edition of *New England's Prospect.*

1637:   The Pequot War pits colonists against Pequot Indians in the first significant racial conflict in New England.

Suggestions for Further Reading

PRIMARY SOURCES

The primary source literature for early English plans for North America is abundant and readily available in most college or university libraries. Perhaps the best place to start is Louis B. Wright's excellent collection of documents, *The Elizabethans' America: A Collection of Early Reports by Englishmen on the New World* (Cambridge: Harvard University Press, 1966); Wright's edition reprints some entire tracts but includes excerpts as well. For the complete edition of virtually every important early work, see David Beers Quinn and Alison O. Quinn, eds. *New American World*, 5 vols. (New York and London: Macmillan, 1979). David Quinn also edited the two-volume *The Roanoke Voyages, 1584–1590* (New York: Dover, 1991), available in paperback. Quinn and Raleigh A. Skelton edited Richard Hakluyt's *The Principall Navigations, Voiages, and Discoveries of the English Nation*, 2 vols. (Cambridge: Cambridge University Press, 1965). There is a paperback facsimile edition of the 1590 illustrated edition of Thomas Harriot's *A Briefe and True Report of the New Found Land of Virginia* (New York: Dover, 1972), which contains an excellent introduction by Paul Hulton. John White's original watercolors, from which de Bry made his prints, are in London in the British Library and the British Museum; they have been reprinted in Hulton's *America 1585: The Complete Drawings of John White* (Chapel Hill: University of North Carolina Press and British Museum Publications, 1984). E. G. R. Taylor, ed. *The Original Writings and Correspondence of the Two Richard Hakluyts*, 2 vols., Works Issued by the Hakluyt Society, 2nd ser., 76–77 (London, 1935), contains more primary source information relating to the Hakluyts and their ventures.

In addition, students can read the writings of other explorers and early colonists in recent editions of their writings. For Captain John Smith, the best place to start is Karen Ordahl Kupperman's *Captain John Smith: A Select Edition of His Writings* (Chapel Hill: University of North Carolina Press, 1988). As Kupperman notes in her preface, "John Smith deserves to be read" (v), and her collection draws from Smith's work to provide his views on such topics as his relation with Indians, his views of the environment, and his thoughts on future colonization efforts. For those interested in reading more of Smith's works, Philip L. Barbour's magnificent collection, *The Complete Works of Captain John Smith*, 3 vols. (Chapel Hill:

University of North Carolina Press, 1986), contains excellent introductions and notes as well as the texts themselves. William Bradford's *Of Plymouth Plantation*, ed. Samuel Eliot Morison (New York: Knopf, 1953), contains his views on Plymouth's early development. Alan Heimert and Andrew Delbanco have brought together a stimulating collection of Puritan writings in *The Puritans in America: A Narrative Anthology* (Cambridge: Harvard University Press, 1985). Alden Vaughan's recent edition of William Wood's *New England's Prospect* (Amherst: University of Massachusetts Press, 1977) contains an excellent introductory essay and notes and has recently been issued in paperback. For a different view of early New England, see Thomas Morton, *New English Canaan*, originally published in London in 1632 and contained in Peter Force, ed. *Tracts and Other Papers, Relating Principally to the Origin, Settlement, and Progress of the Colonies in North America*, 4 vols. (Washington, 1836–1846).

SECONDARY SOURCES

The secondary literature on the topic of colonization is enormous and has received a boost from the recent Columbus Quincentennial. For those interested in the European colonization of North America, perhaps the most logical starting point is J. H. Elliott, *The Old World and the New, 1492–1650* (1970, reprint, Cambridge: Cambridge University Press, 1992), a splendid, if brief, collection of essays. The significance of the Western Hemisphere to Europeans was immense, as is evident in such works as Stephen Greenblatt, *Marvelous Possessions: The Wonder of the New World* (Chicago: University of Chicago Press, 1991), and Anthony Pagden, *European Encounters with the New World* (New Haven: Yale University Press, 1993). One of the most fascinating recent accounts, filled with maps and diagrams from the early modern period, is Valerie Flint's *The Imaginative Landscape of Christopher Columbus* (Princeton: Princeton University Press, 1992).

The history of English westward expansion has been traced with great care in a number of works. For the late medieval precedents, see R. R. Davies, *Domination and Conquest: The Experience of Ireland, Scotland, and Wales, 1100–1300* (Cambridge: Cambridge University Press, 1990). For the early modern push into Ireland and its consequences, the best single work is Nicholas Canny, *The Elizabethan Conquest of Ireland: A Pattern Established, 1565–76* (New York: Barnes and Noble, 1976). There are useful essays on selected aspects of this episode in Ciaran Brady and Raymond Gillespie, eds. *Natives and Newcomers: Essays on the Making of Irish Colonial Society, 1534–1641* (Bungay, Suffolk: Irish Academic Press, 1986); and part 2 of Liam de Paor's *The Peoples of Ireland: From Prehistory to Modern Times* (London: Hutchinson, 1986) which provides a solid overview of the topic.

For works that describe English experiences across the Atlantic and into North America, interested readers should start with David Harris Sacks's marvelous *The Widening Gate: Bristol and the Atlantic Economy, 1450–1700* (Berkeley: University of California Press, 1991). Sacks, perhaps better than any other writer, makes sense of English expansion westward by describing the developing relationship between the English and the resources and peoples of the Atlantic world. David Quinn has also written at great length on the topic and provided an excellent narrative account of European expansion that places English efforts in the wider context necessary for understanding it; see, among his many fine works, *North America from Earliest Discovery to First Settlements: The Norse Voyages to 1612* (New York: Harper and Row, 1975). The environmental implications of European expansion are the subject of Alfred W. Crosby's important *Ecological Imperialism: The Biological Expansion of Europe, 900–1900* (New York: Cambridge University Press, 1986). D. W. Meinig's *The Shaping of America: A Geographical Perspective on 500 Years of History*, vol. 1, *Atlantic America, 1492–1800* (New Haven: Yale University Press, 1986), provides the most solid overview of the geographical issues involved; it is filled with excellent maps. Carl O. Sauer's *Seventeenth Century North America* (Berkeley: Turtle Island, 1980) provides a highly literary geographical interpretation of the period, with a focus on the entire continent and all of the peoples who met during that crucial century.

For studies that focus more specifically on the early period of English colonization in North America, interested readers might want to start with two works by Karen Ordahl Kupperman. *Roanoke: The Abandoned Colony* (Savage, Md.: Rowman and Littlefield, 1984), is an excellent account of the failed English effort to settle modern-day North Carolina; *Settling with the Indians: The Meeting of English and Indian Cultures in America, 1580–1640* (London: S. M. Dent, 1980) provides necessary details for understanding the encounter between Indians along the Atlantic coast and English colonizers. William Cronon's masterful and highly readable study of early New England, *Changes in the Land: Indians, Colonists, and the Ecology of New England* (New York: Hill and Wang, 1983), explores the environmental dimension of contact in that region. Neal Salisbury's *Manitou and Providence: Indians, Europeans, and the Making of New England, 1500–1643* (New York: Oxford University Press, 1980) provides excellent details about the early years of settlement there, with particular attention to the clash of cultures that took place between Indians and the English, especially the Puritans. Readers interested in the Puritan experience might want to start with Edmund Morgan's *Visible Saints: The History of a Puritan Idea* (New York, 1963; reprint, Ithaca: Cornell

University Press, 1965), a fine general introduction to Puritan beliefs. Perry Miller's works on Puritans in New England remain vital; interested readers should in particular consult *The New England Mind: The Seventeenth Century* (1939; reprint, Cambridge: Harvard University Press, 1982), and his collection of essays, *Errand into the Wilderness* (1956; reprint, Cambridge: Harvard University Press, 1981). For those interested in early colonization along the Chesapeake, the place to start is Edmund Morgan's *American Slavery, American Freedom: The Ordeal of Colonial Virginia* (New York: Norton, 1975); the early chapters in particular treat the origins of English settlement in the region.

For readers interested in aspects of Indian history (as opposed to Indian-colonist relations), the Smithsonian Institution Press has issued a number of important works. Among these are the ongoing *Handbook of North American Indians,* under the general editorship of William C. Sturtevant. Of particular interest for the colonization of the east coast are volumes 4, *History of Indian-White Relations,* ed. Wilcomb Washburn (1988) and volume 15, *Northeast,* ed. Bruce Trigger (1978). In addition, John W. Verano and Douglas H. Ubelaker have edited a collection of essays, *Disease and Demography in the Americas* (1992), and Herman J. Viola and Carolyn Margolis have edited *Seeds of Change: A Quincentennial Commemoration* (1991), a lavishly illustrated catalog of a museum show on the long-term consequences of the European colonization of the Western Hemisphere. Readers seeking more information about the demography of Indian America should consult Russell Thornton, *American Indian Holocaust and Survival: A Population History since 1492* (Norman: University of Oklahoma Press, 1987).

Index